The SEED *of* DREAMS

A PRACTICAL GUIDE TO GROWING BOLD VISIONS IN THE GARDEN OF YOUR LIFE

By Chip Richards

The **SEED** *of* **DREAMS**

Published by Blue Gaia World Publishers®
10 Trafford Court, Wheelers Hill,
Victoria, Australia 3150

info@bluegaiapublishing.com
www.bluegaiapublishing.com

Edited by Jules Sutherland and Peter Loupelis
Designed by Gemma Christensen

Blue Gaia World Publishers® is a registered trademark of Namaste Publishers Pty Ltd (ACN: 613 264 476), and part of the Blue Angel Publishing Group.

ISBN: 978-1-922574-23-7

*For Ash and Josh.
Thank you for creating with me
the garden of our precious life.*

You are the most magical seeds of all.

The SEED of DREAMS

INTRODUCTION

The greatest achievement
was, at first and for a time
a dream.

The oak sleeps in the acorn;
the bird waits in the egg;
and in the highest vision of
the soul a waking angel stirs.

Dreams are the
seedlings of reality.

JAMES ALLEN

TĀNE MAHUTA

We lived in New Zealand for a time in the early 2000s on a beautiful property with big ocean views. Most of the trees had been planted 15 years prior and were flowering, mature and well-formed. All except for one. A spindly little sapling that had been planted right smack dab in the middle of the front lawn. It was so sparse and out-of-place looking that we almost considered removing it … until one day, when one of our neighbours spotted it, paused in her tracks and said, "Wow."

I replied, "Yeah, doesn't look very healthy, does she? We don't quite know what to do with it …"

"You know what she's doing, don't you?" She replied.

I didn't.

"It might not look like much is happening on the surface, but right now this tree is growing on the inside. Her root system is spreading deep into the earth and across your entire lawn here, preparing for the tree she will one day become."

"Oh, wow. When will that happen?"

"When she's ready." My neighbour studied the tree for a while, appreciating her tininess. "Probably in twenty to thirty years."

"Twenty or thirty years?! Without growing any bigger than this?"

"Maybe longer actually," she said with a smile. "She'll stay like this until her roots are as big as her canopy will one day become."

She paused for a moment, then winked at me, "But she'll be growing on the inside."

"Ok …" I tried to picture an upside-down tree with branches growing in the earth across our lawn. "How will we know when she's ready to grow … on the outside?"

She paused, taking in the little tree and the ocean vista beyond. Then she looked at me with a big grin. "You'll know … because you'll no longer have an ocean view." This was hard to imagine given the 180-degree view from where were standing. "But you'll be sharing this land with one of the greatest trees on the planet."

SEEDS OF POSSIBILITY

The New Zealand kauri tree is a remnant of the ancient sub-tropic rainforest that once grew in the north island of New Zealand. Kauris spend their first 400–800 years reaching maturity and commonly live to be well over 1000 years old, climbing to 50 metres in height with a trunk of up to five metres in diameter. Tāne Mahuta, known by the Maori as 'God of the Forest', is one of the oldest kauri trees still standing and is thought to be up to 2,500 years old.

Each spring Tāne Mahuta flushes with fresh, bright-green leaves of renewal. In autumn he drops cones full of seeds, each of which hold the perfect blueprint of a future tree. Every seed has potential to find purchase in the soil and begin its journey to becoming the fullest expression of itself in the forest.

It's hard to believe there was a time when even Tāne Mahuta was just a small seed of possibility looking for a place to be planted into the soil of reality and begin. But this is the way many of our dreams—even the epic ones—enter our lives. They arrive as tiny seeds, inklings of ideas, almost unrecognisable amidst the many other thoughts, pressures and expectations in life — except that they carry the whisper of a future vision that is calling us to grow into it.

THE SEED OF THIS DREAM

This book landed in my heart like a kauri seed about 22 years before the time of writing it. It arrived as a tiny, creative impulse with a complete table of contents, ready to be planted. I wrote a draft manuscript, began sharing lessons and metaphors in my work and have continued to feel deeply connected to the vision of this project for many years. But for some reason the manuscript itself sat quietly on the shelf until now — a sapling in the middle of my front garden, seemingly insignificant amidst all the demands and fast-growing impulses of life.

For a long time, I thought I was simply procrastinating (and there were likely elements of that), but each time I revisited the project, I discovered a strange phenomenon … Somehow, even in my absence, the seed of the idea continued to grow. And with each new season of life, my own reflections of each chapter deepened and spread, much like the roots of the young kauri tree in its first 20 years of growth.

During this time, I have had the opportunity to grow and cultivate several actual gardens in different lands and climates, and—as a coach and mentor of athletes, artists and business leaders globally—I have had the gift of supporting the rising development of many bold dreams and visions.

These experiences have left me with a deep appreciation of the parallels between the steps required to cultivate a thriving garden and the steps required to grow a dream to fruition in life.

En route, I've realised that the real seed that has been growing in preparation for the completion of this book, is me.

THE GREATEST RISK OF ALL

After working closely with human potential and gardens for the majority of my life, I have come to believe that each of us comes into this world with unique seeds of boundless potential — dreams and attributes that make up our own unique blueprint, without which the great garden of life would be incomplete. But this is easy to forget.

Just as many of the ancient forests have been lost and many people have stopped growing their own gardens and food, much of humanity has also lost touch with the unique calling that each of us carries deep within us. In efforts to make ends meet and fulfil the roles and expectations that others may have of us, we have forsaken one of our greatest human powers. The power to honour the pulse of our unique visions. The power to dream, and to let ourselves dream big.

In times of change and uncertainty, it can be tempting to restrict our visions. To convince ourselves that perhaps we should save our bigger dreams—the ones we secretly feel most called towards—for another day. Save them for a different season, when the dust has settled, when conditions are better. When we are more ready, more worthy, less stressed, more qualified. But life's churning soil makes fertile ground for new possibilities, and the truth is there has never been a better or more important time to cultivate the power of our dreams.

Of all the crisis in need of our attention on planet Earth, perhaps the most pressing risk of all is the risk of losing touch with the human power to dream new possibilities into reality.

FROM ONE SINGLE SEED

If we think about it, virtually every great work of art, well-crafted novel, thriving business and visionary enterprise began at some level as the seed of a dream. Every ecological breakthrough and bold humanitarian initiative, every pioneering invention and every solution to an unsolvable problem, each began as an idea or spark of inspiration (or irritation!) that germinated in the heart/mind of someone long enough, with enough intensity to begin to sprout and grow roots.

From a single seed, an entire forest is born. From one dream, millions of people are touched. But it all starts here with the one. With you. The seed of potential you are, and the seeds of possibility you carry.

It does not matter right now if you have a clear vision for what you've come here to plant or not. It doesn't matter if you feel like you are at the beginning, the end or somewhere in between. You may have your next big project perfectly mapped out or you may be standing at the crossroads waiting to see what happens next.

It doesn't matter if you are a student or a grandmother, a breakdancer, botanist or business leader (or all of the above). If you're holding this book right now, then I'd say you're in the perfect place to start.

The Seed of Dreams is a simple guide to help those who are ready to answer the call of your dreams, for real. However grand or simple. To honour the unique seeds that you carry and to plant them into the world with energy, love and power.

This book is one of my seeds of a dream that has been growing inside of me, and causing me to grow long enough now, so I'm planting it here with you.

May it serve to churn the soil of your deepest held visions and open a path of discovery and realisation of the dreams that are now ready to come through YOU.

1.

INTEND
(+ CREATE SPACE)

All that you need you have
within you, waiting to be
recognised, developed and
drawn forth.

An acorn contains
within it a mighty oak.
You contain within you
tremendous potential.

Just as the acorn has to
be planted and tended to
enable it to grow and become
that mighty oak, so that
which is within you has to
be recognised before it can
be drawn forth and used to
the full, otherwise it lives
dormant in you.

EILEEN CADDY

My grandfather 'Pops' was an avid gardener. He lived in a one-bedroom inner-city apartment in Evanston, Illinois with not a lot of room (inside or out), but his balcony was filled with potted plants, most of which served a specific role in Pops' cooking. He was a wiry Irishman and a passionate storyteller with wild eyes and the warmest of smiles. Pops had an ability to blend fact with fantasy in a way that left us wanting to believe. And when he cooked, Pops the Irishman became Italian — in voice, movement and mannerisms. So, in those pots on his veranda grew all the specific herbs, spices and tomatoes needed for Pops' family-famous pasta sauces.

Watching him carefully pinch individual leaves of oregano and basil off their plant and listening to him sing to the ripening of tomatoes on the vine was probably my earliest exposure to the growing of seeds. It's also how I instantly recognised the twisted limbs of an aged tomato bush in the dried-up front yard garden bed, the day my wife Ash, our then-one-year-old son Josh and I moved into our first property together in northern New South Wales, Australia.

It was a tired old dairy farm, with a very sweet but tired old farmhouse. The little, rectangular front-yard garden bed—with its tangled tomato bush relic and overgrown weeds—was an echo of what had been there before us and a whispered invitation of what was to come.

During the first few weeks of our time living there, I spent a fair amount of time standing on the creaky old veranda looking out across the front yard to the land and hills beyond. My eyes would often stop on the little garden bed, framed by weathered wooden beams. I would imagine what it would look like full of thriving greens and the flush of fresh vegetables. Over time, my picture of what it could be started to grow and expand, until one day, just before sunset, I felt a compelling urge to pick up my shovel and start digging. I didn't know yet what I was going to plant in there, but I knew that until I cleared out some of the old and prepared the space for new seeds to find purchase, there was very little that would actually fit or have a chance to grow.

I preserved the tomato vine and a couple of small herbs that seemed to wink at me like Pops, but the rest became mulch and part of a process of preparing this bed for the seeds and seedlings that would soon be planted there.

Flash forward 20 years and we now live on a different property (about 40 minutes south) with over 400 different varieties of fruiting trees, herbs, vegetables and other edible, medicinal plants — most of which we have planted since arriving here. My son Josh inherited Pops' passion for Italian food, so we've got all of those herbs growing, as well as an ever-growing depth and variety of foods for different moments and nutritional needs — for humans and bees alike (more on bees later).

But for me, it all started there with the first tiny garden bed of our first little farmlet and a simple moment of genuine intent. A glimmer of open imagining and a willingness to dig the shovel in and create space for something new to emerge.

❧

SEEDS GROW IN SMALL CONTAINERS

Sometimes dreams find a way to wedge their way into our lives, whether we *intend* to give them space or not (just as dandelions grow up through the cracks of sidewalks — more on them later). But if we are going to consciously invite the growth and development of a dream, creating space for it to emerge in our mind and in our life is a great first step.

Some of us postpone this step (the intention to dream) because we think we aren't ready, don't have time, aren't qualified or clear enough to begin. The subconscious thought process might go something like, "I don't know exactly what I want, or if I do, I don't believe it's possible, so I won't consciously intend anything — in case what I get is not what I want and then it's too late to turn back!"

What Pops taught me was that seeds—and dreams—can grow in small containers. In fact, limited space (in the beginning at least) allows us to keep an eye on them and care for them more easily. And what I learned from my own first garden experience is that taking time to survey the landscape, to appreciate what's already growing there and to clear space for what we are ready for, is a key part of inviting what's next.

CREATING SPACE FOR SEEDS TO RISE

When I survey our current garden and the present state of dreams growing in our life, I can see a mix of things growing. Some were consciously planned, planted and carefully nurtured to fruition. Others have emerged naturally from previous seasons of planting and grown into our life garden spontaneously. These include pumpkin seeds from our compost soil now growing randomly at the base of trees, as well as referrals of new business clients arriving unexpectedly from cross-pollinating friends. And while there are aspects of life and garden that are carefully curated into neat, tidy rows (and well-scheduled meetings), there are also fresh creative impulses, unexpected partnerships and vines full of passionfruit weaving their way into places we never previously imagined.

I walk the land each day watering what is needed and harvesting what is ready. I navigate my work schedule, coaching the projects, dreams and aspirations of my clients. I can see that everything growing here, in life and garden, is part of an overall intention that has been set and refined, mulched and reseeded by my family and me throughout our journey together. Many things are growing now that we never would have imagined when we began. Our willingness to **intend**, to create space for what's possible and then to remain open to how life responds to this intention, has been a dance that is both an essential first step and ongoing aspect (highlight) of the dream-growing experience.

When we take time to create space and **intend**, this includes both the things we know and can plan for and things which are 'aligned' with our intent but which we cannot yet imagine, based on where we currently stand. Once we begin taking steps, seedling dreams may arrive from previously unidentified sources, and they may grow in unplanned places … but the power and purpose of clarifying our intent is that we are setting an internal compass and initiating a co-creative process with life. We are shifting from being passive recipients of bird-dropping seeds— knowing some of our best fruit trees may arrive this way—to being conscious ignitors of dreams.

We may not have all the answers. We may not know where this dream will take us or even know exactly where to start. But when we set a clear intention, we are setting into motion a process for bringing something new into life. We are signalling to the Universe we are ready to give, receive and take action in service of our dreams.

THE POWER OF A FEELING

The act of *__intending__* can happen in an overall 'life view' sort of way when we are considering a new direction, a new year, career move or chapter of existence … but it can also happen in a simple way each day when we're planning the focus of our time and how to prioritise our energy and actions.

Even in our busiest times, when people need and expect things from us, there is always time to take at least one deep breath (or maybe two), survey the landscape before us and to ask the deeper part of ourselves, "Amidst everything I am hoping to 'do' today, if I could achieve one thing well and emerge with an overall feeling from the day, what would that be? What is my most important *calling* for today? What is my ultimate intent?"

You may not know the exact specifics of what is going to happen or how you will get there, but you can get clear about how you want to feel. This feeling will grow in you like a seed of intention, guiding and informing your actions in ways both logical and mystical. What happens next will be clearer, more empowered and fruitful as a result, every time.

When we set a clear
intention, we are setting
into motion a process
for bringing something
new into life.

REFLECTION

- If you were to consider your own life right now as if it were a garden, how would you describe it?

- How is the garden of your life currently laid out?

- Is it organised and well-tended, or sprawling and out of control?

- Is it thriving with food for all to share, or parched and in need of heavy rainfall, sunlight or care?

- If you considered the different aspects of who you are and how you channel your gifts and intentions in the world, what dreams are already growing in and around you? Take a moment to appreciate these parts of you that are already emerging and expressing in the world.

- What would you love more than anything to create space for in the garden of your dreams? If there was one thing you could grow more of in your life right now, what would that be?

ACTION

1. Create space to grow something new in your life and ***intend*** to do it.

    ◆ Ask yourself what you would most love to grow to fruition in your life at this time and take time to listen for the answer. Write it down.

2. As a symbol of your willingness to grow something new in your life, find a physical area in your immediate surroundings that you could grow a new plant, tree or garden of some type.

3. Start this week by clearing and creating space to grow this new plant or garden bed. It doesn't matter if you have acres of land or a studio apartment. Just imagine what would be the ultimate outcome, and begin.

2.

ACCEPT
(THE GIFT OF A SEEDLING DREAM)

Wisdom begins
in wonder.

SOCRATES

There is a moment when a seed that has been lying dormant in the ground first cracks open to throw its first shoot or tiny root. It's a subtle moment, often unnoticed, but it is very significant. It is a birthing moment. Months or years may pass before this seed will grow into full expression, but it is here in this moment that we get our first glimpse of a new plant or tree in motion.

In life, sometimes we catch a glimpse of future possibilities when a seedling dream first arrives in our mind or experience. It may be just a flash moment or an idea but in that moment a pulse of clarity strikes at the core of our being. It's the very beginning, and like a small seed in its first moments of germination, it could be overlooked or shaded out. But if we do notice, if we take interest and create space for this seedling to grow, we will one day look back and recognise this moment as a defining one. A moment in which a seed of new possibility was first planted into the soil of our reality.

❧

When I was nine years old, my dad followed a business dream in the financial planning industry and moved our family from the flat lands of Wisconsin into the mountains of Colorado. We moved into our new house on a Friday evening in winter, and on Saturday morning my dad loaded me and my brothers on a bus to the closest major ski resort, about an hour away. As the youngest of three boys, I had been pulled into a myriad of team and ball sports since before I could stand, but I had never stood on a mountain … and I had never skied.

I remember feeling nauseous from the diesel fumes in the back of the bus. I remember the stiffness of ski boots and the awkward clanking of skis and poles being carried together. I remember the white light of mountain sun and the wet numbness on my face. I remember my older brothers heading off for their lessons further up the mountain.

*(They had done this before, leaving me in phase one of 'ski school'.)
And I remember the quiet rush of my very first ski run down the front
side of the mountain. Awkward, tense, focused and quite out of control.
And in that moment, something inside of me woke up.*

*That night, I stood up at the family dinner table and declared that skiing
was my new favourite thing to do in life. In fact, I was pretty sure it was
my main reason for being here.*

*Little did I know that five years later, I would be standing at that same
dinner table declaring to my family that I had decided I was going to
go to the Olympics in the sport of freestyle skiing — even though at the
time I was only just beginning to compete! Or that five years after that,
I would actually be ranked #1 in the sport in the US, with my eyes
fixed firmly on World Cup and Olympic qualification. I didn't know
that my path as an athlete would be radically interrupted by a series of
joint-exploding injuries right at the pinnacle of my career. I didn't know
that this painful interruption would nudge me to discover the path of
coaching, which would lead me a few years later to Australia as the head
coach of the Olympic team here.*

*As that nine-year-old beginner, I had no idea that the dream I was
planting would grow into anything at all, let alone a career path
coaching elite athletes, leaders, teams, artists and businesses from around
the world … Or that this journey would bring me the even greater gift of
meeting my wife Asheyana, igniting our life together, the birth of our son
Josh and the growing of land, animals, gardens and dreams on this side
of the world.*

*As that nine-year-old in the kitchen, holding the tiny seed of a new
dream, there was no way I could have imagined the life journey that
continues to grow to this day from that single moment.*

The ability to qualify for, receive, and act on personal revelation is the single most important skill that can be acquired in this life.

JULIE B. BECK

IT ALL BEGINS SOMEWHERE

When you survey the garden of your life as it is right now, it may be powerful to consider that pretty much everything that is growing there is doing so because it was sparked as an idea, given energy and allowed to grow there.

The people you have in your life, the work you are doing, the projects and hobbies you are immersed in — they all began as an impulse, an idea. If they are growing in your life, it is because you've planted them there (consciously or subconsciously) and enabled them to do so. Even the things you don't consciously *want* to **accept** in your life — the things you'd like to change, let go of or grow out of — normally don't just arrive there on their own. If they do, they don't stick around without us giving them energy and space to grow.

Because life is full and moving at such a rapid pace, we may find ourselves with a combination of things we consciously chose to create and things that unconsciously arrived there, often along with other people's opinions or expectations of us. We can end up so busy reacting to the pull of the most pressing needs and responsibilities around us that we don't take time to consciously listen or consider — what is the dream that most wants to grow through us or be planted in our life now?

But if we did, and when we do, we find that there are indeed seeds inside of us, waiting their turn — unique gifts, loaded energy and inspired ideas that are all our own. Often, they are in fact already here, growing quietly without us even recognising them. So close that we don't appreciate them for the gifts they are ready to bring or already bringing.

INNATE GIFTS

A business-owner friend of mine is studying to be a stand-up comedian. I listened to him give a speech about the process of learning to be funny, how self-conscious and uncomfortable he is on stage. While he was humbly explaining his journey and how difficult it was to make people laugh (at this stage, not trying to be funny at all), he was delightfully surprised to look up and see everyone in stitches laughing. He had spent so much time thinking about the things he thought he needed to do in order to 'become a comedian', that he almost missed discovering how funny he was simply by being himself.

My wife Ash has unmeasurable creative superpowers that express themselves freely in pretty much every area of her life. The way she moves, eats, dresses, sculpts clay, designs a room, communicates with animals and articulates truth to a friend in need — all happen effortlessly, with deep creativity. But when it comes time to channel that energy in the direction of her 'dream' as a painter she often feels like she lacks the creative clarity, skills or knowledge to start. Looking on from the outside, as she creates beautiful painting after painting, is like watching an eagle that is already soaring, trying to figure out how to fly.

In this way, often our dreams — and the powers we require to fulfil them — are right here, hiding deep within who we are. We may need to uncover or unravel them. We may need to cultivate new skills and expand our view and approach. We may be stimulated by external events but one of the greatest gifts most dreams will give us is not to be found 'out there', but rather the discovery of what is already here resting, growing, ready to rise from within.

When we have created intention to honour the seeds which are ours to grow, and when we lean in to hear what they have to say, our dreams do have a way of speaking up and revealing themselves to us.

Our job is to listen, to be open to receiving the rising energy of a seedling dream, and to ***accept*** it.

THE POWER OF LISTENING

Even if we don't know where it came from, why it has arrived or where it may ultimately lead. Even if we don't yet have the skills or knowledge to get where the dream may be calling us to go — the first step is simply being willing to listen, hear and ***accept*** that the dream has come to us. And it has done so for a reason.

Sometimes we don't ask the question or give ourselves permission to listen for the answer because we are nervous of what we might hear — or that we might not hear anything at all.

In my experience, asking ourselves to reveal a dream is a bit like looking east to see the sunrise. We may have to wait a little while. It may seem like it actually gets darker first. Sometimes the light is enshrouded. But if we stand at the water's edge or the mountain ledge looking east, and if we are willing to wait upon it, the sun will always rise.

The answer may not come as you imagine it would and the timing may not be as you expect it. But the dreams that are waiting to come through you will always look for their moment to be seen, to be heard and to begin.

DREAMS HAVE SEASONS

Part of learning to ***accept*** the gift of a seedling dream is to recognise that we cannot always control the timing or the way it grows. These seeds are ours to carry and cultivate, but each seed has a timing all its own.

Different seasons are right for different seeds. And sometimes dreams come to us in unlikely packages.

As I'm typing these words, I can see a stack of seed envelopes on the other side of my studio. Seeds that we've purchased from local nurseries and others we've collected post-harvest (more on this later) here on our land. As we move into autumn, some of these seeds (broccoli, cauliflower, mustard greens) are primed for planting now, but others (cucumber, tomatoes, zucchini) will simply need to wait for spring before they have the best chance to grow. I can influence their development to a certain degree with the conditions I give them, but part of my role as the gardener is to pay attention to the seasons and to listen for what is ready to grow now. To give direct, committed energy to the seeds that are right for this season, and to resist forcing those that are not.

In life, there is our preferred timing and there is the natural unfolding of the dream. There are dreams that we want to grow and there are dreams that want to grow through us. Sometime these two are the same, but sometimes they are different. It's up to us to be open to receiving the gift of a seedling dream even if it doesn't look like the dream that we thought that we wanted to grow.

When my peaking growth as an athlete was chopped down to earth by devastating injury two seasons in a row, it was painful for me to consider that the dream I had invested all of my time, energy and passion into was not the dream that life had in store for me. Looking back now at the incredible life garden that has grown as a result of my personal dream ending, I can see there was a natural changing of seasons unfolding all along. While it would have been impossible for me to imagine the wider dreams that were being seeded into my life at the time of my injuries, I can recognise that part of being able to powerfully 'move on' was to open myself to **accept** the gift of the seedling dream — even when it didn't look like I thought it would.

ACCEPTING YOUR MISSION

If you were to give yourself just a moment right now to ask the question, "What seedling dream is now ready to grow in/through me …?", and if you took a few minutes to really, honestly listen, what answer would you hear?

Amidst all that is supposed to get done, if there was one dream you feel most called to fulfil at this time, in this season, what would it be?

What would it look like to **accept** this into your life as a genuine living thing, ready to be planted and to grow?

By asking ourselves to home in on the essence of a dream, we are developing a different sort of muscle in our mind, heart and actions — one that learns to recognise and honour the importance of a deeper inner calling. Trying to identify this in an overall life-sense can be a little intimidating. One way to begin honing this muscle is to simply tune in on a micro level each day to ask, listen and respond, "What is the most important mission or mini-dream for my day today? What is here, ready to come through into fruition, just waiting for me to open my eyes and **accept**?"

REFLECTION

- Can you think of a time when a seedling dream arrived in your life in a way that you may not have expected or initially recognised? What allowed you to see it and put it into action in your life?

- Scanning the landscape of your current life, what new possibility is now growing there quietly, waiting to be fully recognised and embraced?

ACTION

1. Identify what is ready to grow in your garden.

    - What plants, fruits or vegetables would you love to grow and could you grow in the current conditions? Buy some and get ready to grow!

2. Identify what is ready to grow in your life.

    - What season is it for you in your life?

    - If there was one dream you feel most called to pursue or fulfil at this time, what would that be?

    - What would it look like to accept this dream as yours to carry, nurture and grow in the world (even if you don't yet know 'how')?

3.

BELIEVE
(IN ITS NECESSITY)

The future belongs to those who believe in the beauty of their dreams.

ELEANOR ROOSEVELT

We used to have a neighbour named Bob. Bob was a retired ex-postman, turned banana farmer with an interesting business model …

During the first three weeks of each month, Bob would drive his ancient tractor house-to-house through our valley, delivering free bags of bananas to all his neighbours, pausing for a chat, lending a hand where needed — from fixing fences, to removing poisonous snakes from places they were not supposed to be. On the fourth week of each month, Bob would load up his truck with boxes of all the remaining bananas and deliver them to a wholesale market. I'm not sure how profitable Bob's business was in terms of money, but in the currency of goodwill and kindness, Bob was one of the wealthiest men I've ever met.

In our early days living on the land, Bob was like a farm-life superhero to us. He could make, fix or grow just about anything. Whenever he was given a challenge that seemed to have no answer, or whenever we called him over to help us fix one of ours (often) he'd close his eyes in thought for a moment and then sort of snap awake with a grin and say, "There's always a way."

When I started preparing my first garden bed for planting, Bob used to drop by with my weekly banana delivery and watch me dig. Sometimes he'd throw a few suggestions my way. Once we started planting, he'd occasionally bring me a seedling plant from his own garden. It would usually be in a small cardboard box or takeaway coffee cup, held snug with a handful of soil. He wouldn't make a big deal about it—he'd usually tell me he stole it from his wife Margaret—but as he handed it to me there was always a small moment of seriousness, as though he was handing me a golden egg. He'd ask a couple qualifying questions to make sure I knew how to care for it, he'd look me deep in the eye for a moment, and then he'd break into that postman-banana-farmer smile, "Alright then. I better get home before I get in trouble." He'd sputter the old tractor to a start and head off down the driveway.

I'd usually pop the little seedling onto a protected shelf on our veranda where I could water it and protect it from the elements until it was ready to go in the ground. Bob would never mention the gift again, but I knew he would be quietly watching and occasionally I'd catch his eyes pausing on the seedlings with an approving nod once they were planted in the garden. Like a grandfather might gaze upon a young child learning a new skill.

On my side of the exchange, when Bob handed me a seedling and I took it into my hands, I felt a strange sort of transference of responsibility. There was no stated obligation, just a quiet sort of knowing in the exchange. Even though it was only a tiny little plant, somehow I knew it was important. Important enough to keep it watered and safe until it was ready to go into the ground. And important enough to look after it closely once it was in.

❦

THE MANY FACES OF SEEDLING DREAMS

In life, seedling dreams come to us in many forms, and they arrive in all sorts of moments. A fresh creative impulse bubbles up while driving through the city, an inspired business idea bounces into form during a late-night talk with a friend, a whispered vision finds you repeatedly during morning walks on the beach …

Sometimes seedling dreams literally show up as a gift — a first guitar for a future musician, a blank canvas to an aspiring artist. Sometimes they come in a single moment or experience — a future pro surfer stands up on her first wave, future life partners meet eyes for the first time. And sometimes seedling dreams are masked upon arrival, disguised as unexpected, often inconvenient, interruptions to what we had originally 'planned'. Many doctors and naturopaths begin their journey toward supporting the vitality of others after experiencing a personal health crisis. Many environmental and humanitarian pioneers begin the mission to serve their cause after personally confronting the same issue.

Yachtsman Ian Kiernan began a local water clean-up that became the nationwide Clean Up Australia and Clean Up the World organisations following a yacht race that exposed him to unfathomable amounts of rubbish in the sea. Virgin Airlines was born in the mind of Richard Branson while navigating the frustrations of a cancelled flight. My own seedling dream as a coach arrived in the form of major injury after pushing too hard towards my own high-performance pursuits. Often the medicine we need to nurture the dream seeds that call us come from the experiences we have enroute to discovering them.

In whatever form the dream arrives, whether in a moment of lightning bolt inspiration, frustration or crisis, whether clear and simple or difficult to recognise, when we look back years later, we will often recognise this experience as a defining moment. A moment when a dream seed is first planted into the soil of our reality.

In some cultures, it is believed that stories and great works of art carry with them a living essence that seeks expression in the world. I have come to believe the same is true of dreams. We often think that we are the seekers and inventors of dreams, but it is powerful to consider that the dreams we are seeking may also be seeking us — whispering through our experiences, shaping and nudging us to answer their call and bring them through.

Like seeds, dreams are living entities that have a lifeline and journey to fulfil. When we *accept* the gift of a seedling dream and *believe* in its importance, we are acknowledging that this dream has chosen to come to us for a reason. We become a part of its journey, and the dream becomes part of ours.

When Bob gave me a seedling, it was clear and simple. There was no grey zone there. I knew it was important, but even still, these little plants and life forms needed to sit for a while on our veranda before they were ready to be planted in our garden. Similarly, when our dreams arrive in miniature form, in our minds or otherwise, they may need to percolate and mature for a while before being fully planted into our life.

And sometimes in life, it's not as clear and simple to see them sitting there on the shelf or the veranda. But deep inside we often feel them, sense them growing — or wanting to grow — in our mind.

MAKING YOUR DREAM IMPORTANT

Whatever you **believe** in most will get your energy. Whatever gets your energy will grow.

Making a new dream important may require time, energy and commitment. You may need to develop new skills, capacity or levels of focus. It may even cause disruption in your current life to be able to **accept** and grow that which is ready to be planted.

Have you ever had an opportunity arrive in your life in a way that disrupted the 'current plan' but ultimately revealed itself to be exactly what you needed?

Making a new dream important may require you to change your priorities and shift your commitments. It may require building new relationships or pulling back from others. As your **belief** in your dream seed grows, you may even find the need to stand alone for a time, without the input, opinions or expectations of others.

This is not to say that your dreams won't involve, be connected to or serve the dream gardens of others. In fact, many of us have dreams that are directly related to and woven into the dreams of other people.

But it is important to recognise that there are certain dreams that
you alone are here to carry, **believe** in and care for before bringing into
the world.

When it's just a tiny idea swimming in a big, busy life, the young dream
may not seem as urgent or pressing as the current demands on your
energy in other arenas, so it may be easy to think that it does not require
your focus. Or to justify putting it off to another day, year or stage of
life. In truth, when a dream seed is small it may not require an immense
amount of time or energy. Much like the young seedlings Bob gave me, a
little daily water and sunshine was all that was required at first. But as we
make our seedling dreams important, as we give them our focus and our
belief in what they may someday become … they begin to grow.

Cherish your visions and your dreams as they are the children of your soul, the blueprints of your ultimate achievements.

NAPOLEON HILL

REFLECTION

- Consider something you previously believed in strongly enough that it propelled you into real, committed action.

  - What made you believe in it? What did it feel like to move with this belief? What were the results?

- Now consider an area that you would love to make a change or a dream you would love to realise, but until now you may not have believed enough in its importance to make it happen.

- What has stopped you from believing in it or making it important enough to take real action? What risks, sacrifices or costs have you associated with following this dream?

- Looking forward, if you never believed enough to make this dream important, what would happen to it? What would it cost you (or the garden of your life) if you never give this dream an opportunity to grow to fruition?

- Sit quietly for a moment and hold this dream in your mind as though it were a precious seedling in your hands. If this dream had a voice, what would it tell you today? What would it ask of you? What could it one day become if nurtured with real action, from now to fruition? What potential good could come (for you and all involved) if you gave yourself permission to fully **accept** and **believe** in the importance of this dream?

ACTION

1. Identify a seedling, plant or tree that you ***believe*** in enough to make important. Begin to care for it like a living being that has been given to you to nurture.

2. Identify one dream or area of your life that has been waiting for you to ***believe*** in enough to make it important. Hold this dream in your thoughts for a few minutes each day this week as though it were a growing seedling waiting to be planted in your garden. Listen to whatever simple instructions it may give you … and follow them with committed action. Make your dream important. ***Believe*** in its necessity.

4.

PREPARE
(TO GROW)

The secret of change is to focus all of your energy, not on fighting the old, but on building the new.

DAN MILLMAN

The first tree I ever planted was a macadamia tree. As a young family we loved 'macas' but they were really expensive, so we thought hey, let's grow them instead! The region we live in is ideal for growing macadamias and they're a beautiful-looking tree, so it seemed like a no-brainer. We bought a nice mature sapling, I picked a spot in the middle of our field that we would love to one day have a giant, expansive, nut-giving tree, I grabbed my shovel, walked down past our neighbours' cows (who were grazing on our land), dug a hole, transferred him over and watered him in. Done. Dream in motion!

I walked back up the hill quite proud of myself for the immediate transfer of an idea into action. Inspired by the tree this little sapling would one day become. Imagining the tire swing and tree fort Josh and I would one day build in its branches. As I reached our front veranda, I turned back around to admire my handywork, just in time to watch Solomon the bull take his second and last bite of the young tree, snapping the trunk and pulling it front the ground by its the roots. Dream destroyed!

❧

In the garden, there are some simple steps of preparation that quite profoundly impact not only the enjoyment of the process but also the outcome and yield of what we plant there. The same is true for growing dreams.

There are two key arenas we want to think about when we **prepare** for both gardens and dreams. The first is the stuff we need to do on the outside to **prepare** the soil of our garden and the situation of our life in order to grow something new. The second part—less obvious but equally, if not more important—is what we need to do to **prepare** ourselves on the inside (our thoughts, beliefs, commitments) for the lasting change we are seeking to create.

PREPARING THE GROUND (ON THE OUTSIDE)

We've been growing food for a while now, but until a few years ago, we had always done it quite haphazardly, mostly off to the side, along the edges of our field — adding a new bed of lettuce or row of kale as needed through the seasons. We loved the garden, but it was really just a hobby. If nothing was in season in our garden, we wouldn't think twice about buying what we wanted from the store.

Interestingly, you could say that during this time much of the focus and commitment we gave to our dreams was quite similar. We were working hard and achieving positive outcomes in our work, but the quiet dreams we valued the most were often the last things to receive our energy or focus. They were growing slowly, but only 'around the edges' — late at night or very early in the morning (if we had time or energy), before or after the busy schedule of our days.

Growing food was exciting to talk about, but buying groceries was the main thing happening. Cultivating dreams was exciting to think about, but working day-to-day outside of our dreams was the main thing happening.

When we decided to take our food-growing mission to a new level, we didn't realise this step would not only revolutionise our garden, it would also cause a radical recalibration of the focus and commitment we bring to our dreams. Bringing both from the edges, right to the centre of our world.

For the garden side of things, it started with a visit from our friend Joel who is a master of permaculture.

Walking the property with Joel was like entering a training session with a master coach for the first time. He confirmed we had solid raw potential—great soil, good position, plenty of sun—and he appreciated that we had been growing food 'as a hobby', but he challenged us to take it to take it to the next level. He said, "With the right preparation and a bit of focused effort, you guys could actually be growing 90 per cent of your food right here."

We got excited and said, "Great! Let's get planting!"

As Joel started mapping out the steps to set up a 12 x 9 metre 'market garden' right smack-dab in the centre of our field, I was imagining we'd be talking about what seeds to buy and how to tend the different crops … but interestingly about 90% of Joel's focus was on the simple but essential things we needed to do before we could even think about what we wanted to grow. This involved laying thick tarps over the entire area for four to six weeks to kill off all grass and weeds, tilling the soil, letting it rest, building the rows into quadrants, planning crop rotation and growing seedlings mature enough to go into the ground, (to name a few steps).

As I added up the time these steps were going to take, two things happened. Firstly, I realised I had never put real forethought or preparation into the gardens we'd grown in the past, and I started to understand why perhaps our results were hit and miss. Secondly, I began stressing out because it seemed like it would not be days but months before we even put a single seedling into the ground.

"Don't worry," said Joel. "If we set up well, we do it once. Before you know it, you'll have so much food growing here, you'll have to set up a market stall on the street. You will have a food garden you can add to for life."

Flash forward about three months and Joel was right. By spring, we were not only infusing every meal with baskets full of fresh magic from the garden, we were literally sending every friend, house visitor, garden worker and even total strangers home with big bags of fresh veggies every time anyone stopped by or came near our land.

As we went through the process to prepare the land to receive, nurture, feed and support the hundreds of new plants we would one day add to the garden, we began to realise that similar steps are needed to prepare our lives for the dreams we are inspired to create.

❧

This doesn't mean we need to quit our day job or go on sabbatical to write a book, but it does mean we have to be willing to bring our dream from the edges of our life right into the centre. It means we have to create space in our life to give it our most committed energy —and its very best chance to grow.

When Joel was scanning our property for where to put the market garden, he wasn't thinking about how to fit it in with how we'd always done things. He wasn't interested in keeping this garden 'around the edges'. His mind was focused purely on the elements needed (sun, soil, position, etc.) to set up the garden for absolute success — feeding the family and bees while being as central and accessible as possible. When we embark upon a new dream, it's important to consider the same.

PREPARING THE GROUND (ON THE INSIDE)

When we decided to be more deliberate and committed in our food-growing mission, some of the preparation was the physical stuff we had to do. But the longer-term challenge was preparing our minds and bodies to commit to follow through with the path we had chosen.

It's romantic to talk about growing your own food, but the truth is that it is super dynamic and demanding physical work. It requires steady vigilance, consistent focus, collaboration, adaptation, failure, breakthrough, sweat and dirt. Plus, in areas like this where the soil is rich, things grow really fast and then you have to figure out what to do with it all when it's ripe. What does a family of three do with 80 ripe lettuces?!

Interestingly, as we started to fully lean into the food growing mission, what began to surface in our minds was all the areas of life where we were not giving this level of full-focused energy and commitment to set up the projects, visions or creative ideas we had been growing on edges. Unfinished paintings, sculptures and books, entrepreneurial visions and collaborative ideas — all of which had massive potential to grow but were currently just not receiving ample space, soil or sunlight to do so.

Just as seedlings need a well-prepared and fertile garden bed in which to thrive, our dreams need clear space, genuine encouragement and focused energy to develop, so that when they are watered, they too (like our garden) will explode into life.

Dreams are the seeds of change. Nothing ever grows without a seed, and nothing ever changes *without a dream.*

DEBBY BOON

THE MASTERS OF BEE-ING PREPARED

The greatest masters of preparation that I have ever met, who we learn from immensely day-to-day, are the bees.

For many of us, when we think of bees, we can imagine the busyness of the hive, the foraging for nectar and pollen and of course, the magic of honey. As we look a little closer, we discover a highly synchronised, highly organised, masterfully orchestrated and well-prepared community (50–80,000 per hive), each of whom have their own unique purpose and ever-evolving role in service to the whole.

Bees work from pre-dawn until dusk and fly up to five miles each day to find and collect nectar for the hive. While each individual bee only produces approximately one twelfth of a teaspoon of honey in her entire four-to-six-week life, collectively and together, each hive is capable of producing and storing between 60 and 100 pounds of honey each year, which is used to nurture the young and feed the queen and colony through good times and bad. When the balance of life is abundant, there's usually some honey there for the beekeeper too.

When we contemplate this immense cycle of production, one thing that is easy to overlook is the essential step that must be taken before the bees can harvest and store even one single drop of honey.

> *QUESTION: How do the bees **prepare** to receive all of the nectar and pollen that they collect?*
>
> *ANSWER: The bees must first build the honeycomb.*

Honeycomb is a mass of three-dimensional, hexagonal beeswax cells built by the worker bees inside the hive. The wax is created by eight special glands in the bees' abdomen, then chewed together with a little bit of nectar and pollen to form the final substance, capable of being warmed and then collaboratively shaped into a prismatic wall of hexagons. This is the strongest shape in nature, able to hold the most volume of liquid with the least amount of material. Stacked three-dimensionally and double-sided, in perfect symmetry, a frame or bar of honeycomb is an engineering masterpiece which becomes the incubation and birthing ground for future bee generations and can hold and store honey perfectly for 5,000+ years.

*So, while the bees absolutely require the nectar, honey and pollen to survive, they also know they must first meticulously set themselves and their environment up to receive and store it. The effort and work it takes to draw the comb is their way to **prepare** for the rich abundance of life that will then be captured and held there.*

☙

During our dreaming phase, it is easy to become fixated on the outcome (win the client, grow the business, enjoy the nectar) as the primary measure of progress and success, but if this is a dream worth fulfilling to its ultimate potential, it's powerful to consider that an equally important progress measure is how well we ***prepare*** ourselves on the inside and out to receive the thing we are dreaming to create.

When you think about the dreams that are now ready to grow and evolve through you, what would it look like for you to genuinely ***prepare*** yourself and your life to receive them? What would it look like for you to 'draw the comb' so that the nectar you gather with your efforts will be put to its very best use?

To ***prepare*** doesn't mean we perfectly see and plan every single step from the beginning. If we tried to foresee every twist and turn, we could spend years 'preparing' without planting a single seed. This is not the idea. Preparing simply means we make the dream important enough to give it the space and energy it needs to grow. To honour our commitment to the dream not only by going after it, but by building structures in our life to receive it and give it the very best chance to flourish.

REFLECTION

- What would it look like to pull your dream from the private edges of your life garden and make it a central part of your daily focus?

- If you were to take the time to genuinely ***prepare*** as the bees do, to build and receive your dream, what would that look like in practical terms in your life? What would become possible as a result?

- How would you 'draw the honeycomb' of your dream?

ACTION

1. This week, devote some time to preparing a physical space to grow a new plant or tree in. It could be a raised bed, potted plant or full-scale garden in the field. Whatever it is, make it 'central' (not on the edges) and consider what conditions will enable whatever you plant to thrive.

2. This week, devote time to setting up a physical space (i.e., an office or room) and block out time (in your calendar) specifically to focus on growing and developing your dream. When this dream is growing and flourishing in the centre of your life, what kind of space, commitment, focus and belief will you give it then? Start with the end in mind and ***prepare*** to plant your dream into reality.

5.

PLANT
(IN FERTILE GROUND, FOR THE GOOD OF ALL)

Now is the accepted time, not tomorrow, not some more convenient season.

It is today that our best work can be done and not some future or future year.

It is today that we fit ourselves for the greater usefulness of tomorrow.

Today is the seed time, now are the hours of work, and tomorrow comes the harvest.

W.E.B. DU BOIS

About eleven years before the time of this draft, we were trying to find our 'home' in a deep sense of the word. It had been several years since we had sold our last property and during that time I had travelled extensively for work. We had moved several times both in Australia and internationally. Our son Josh was entering his teens and moving toward high school, and we could feel the need to root down and have a base for all of us to sink into and grow. We didn't know where or how exactly, but we felt home was calling us. We had a list of things we imagined ourselves building and growing 'on our land' (fruit trees, a garden for humans and bees, art studio, film studio, etc.). But at that stage, we had no place to plant this vision and no certainty how to get there, geographically, financially or otherwise. Almost nothing about the dream seemed realistic, but something inside of us knew we had to begin.

Of the many steps we started taking to build energy towards the dream, one compelling urge we followed was to begin growing seedlings of the fruit trees we imagined we would one day plant on our envisioned land.

Every time we passed a plant or sapling tree at the farmers market or nursery that we thought we'd love to grow in our future garden, we'd collect it and start caring for it on the back porch. When we ate an especially delicious mango, avocado, lemon or cherry, we'd pop those seeds into a pot of soil with a promise that if it grew, we would one day plant it in the ground.

Over the coming months, an eclectic baby orchard grew on the back patio of our rented apartment until there was literally no place to stand. Each time we watered, it felt like we were watering the seeds of a future that we were in the process of creating together with these seedlings. In a strange way it began to feel like these little seedlings were not only ingredients of our desired outcome, they were also playing a role in our quest to find it!

By the time we found and purchased our property (about 18 months later), we had cultivated an entire moving truck full of young trees and seedlings. These became the founding members of the food garden and orchard on our land.

Flash forward to the present. This morning as I walk through multitude of fruiting trees and countless varieties of edible plants, herbs and vegetables—along with an evolving field of flowering trees and bushes to feed the thousands of bees, birds and pollinators that now live and work together across the property—I feel an indescribable sense of gratitude for the tiny little saplings whose outreaching buds caught our eye from their little pots at the market years ago and the magic role they played in helping us find the sanctuary we all now call home.

Many of these trees—the guavas, tamarillos, Panama berries and citrus (to name a few)—are now producing hundreds of ripe fruit and thousands of new seeds each year, some of which have already become seedlings and saplings of fresh plants and trees, thriving in other parts of our garden and shared with neighbours to plant in theirs.

Looking back, I can see that what was happening during the period of our home quest was a preparation phase for both the dream of finding our home and for the garden we would **plant** *and grow here!*

As I walk around this morning, I am struck with three realisations:

As potted seedlings, these trees fed and inspired our dreams on the inside and out.

They helped us clarify the vision we were committed to creating (what type of land do we need to host all of these plants?) which enabled us to recognise this home as a suitable one for all of us when we found it.

When we have taken the time to **intend** and to **accept** the seedling dreams that want to grow through us, when we **believe** enough to make them important and we have taken time to **prepare** ourselves and our life to grow this dream to fruition, the next vitally essential step is for us to **plant** it into the world with our actions.

THE POWER OF ACTION

Like the seedlings of our garden which start their life in small pots with the protection of our porch—safe from the wind, heavy rains and harsh elements—the early days of growing a dream also requires a safe place to develop, free from the judgment and opinions of the world around us. But just like the seedling plant, whose roots will eventually become bound and restricted inside its pot, there comes a time when, in order for our dreams to survive and bear fruit, we must **plant** them into the garden of our life.

Built into the simple act of purchasing or planting a seed in a pot is a promise to nurture, protect and one day liberate its lifeforce into the earth. This moment of transition from pot to earth can be a risky one for plants, exposing the young seedling to the forces of nature — wind, rain, frost, scorching sun and pests! But without taking this step, the seedling will never fulfil its true potential.

Similarly, the transition between quietly cultivating a dream or idea
in our mind, journal or conversations into genuine committed action
toward its fulfilment, can feel like a risky one. When we step from
the safety of our private dream into action, we expose ourselves to the
dangers of falling short, being judged or getting lost along the way.
But when the time is right, the dream requires this risk of us. It must
be planted into the soil of reality through our actions.

We are the arms and legs of the great creative forces of the Universe.
We are the caretakers of seeds. Our willingness to take action and *plant*
these seedling dreams into the world is the difference between a great
idea that withers away in our mind and a grounded vision that thrives
to inspire many. Between the acorn that sits slowly rotting on the shelf
and the flourishing oak tree that stands, grows and provides for many
generations to come.

Each step of preparation may have been critically important, but there
is a moment when not a single additional second of planning, analysis
or big-picture visioning will help grow your dream. There is a moment
indeed, when the only thing that will move your dream further toward
fruition is for you to *plant* it with your action in the world.

This is your moment!

Luckily, there are some great guiding clues from the garden that can be
helpful — both with our seedlings and our dreams.

CONDITIONS: SETTING YOUR DREAM UP FOR SUCCESS

If we've done the work to *prepare* to grow (Chapter 4), planting our
dreams into action can be a simple and beautiful process. In the garden
world, this means cultivating and choosing the spot that is going to

give the seedling the greatest chance to thrive. A spot with soil that is rich with biomatter, with enough space to breathe and grow, a spot that receives the right amount of sun and shade without too much of either, a spot that is protected from high winds, pests and anyone who might accidentally trample, prematurely pick or mistake them for a weed (more on weeds later). It means planting close to a source of water, with a genuine commitment not to leave it there unattended, but to care for it, to follow it through, to be willing to adapt and grow in your approach alongside the dream.

In life, this means setting our young dream up in an environment that will help it build momentum and grow at the right pace and depth for it to survive. Making sure the physical place where we work on our dream and the mental space we give it are fresh and full of the right energy and nutrients needed for our dream to thrive. Even if this dream is growing as a side project at first (in the 'dream nursery'), if we want it to grow, we need to make sure it receives enough of our focused attention to feed and honour the heartbeat of its potential. Part of making the dream important is giving ourselves the time and space to fully focus on it — even if it is only a little time at first.

In other words, if we don't deliberately schedule it, it won't happen.

Dreams do have a way of continuing to grow in the quiet spaces between our efforts, but we cannot completely ignore a dream or only come to it after everything else is done. Especially while it is young, we must make sure the dream is not completely shaded out by the canopy of more established elements and activities in our life. We have to interrupt the normal patterns if we want something extraordinary to come through. When we ***plant*** it, we must also give the dream space and conditions to grow.

These early actions are really between the dream grower and the dream, and we want to make sure the action of ***planting*** is clear, connected and undiluted. We are building confidence and strength with each step in these early days. We need to be in a safe space to listen, to see and recognise what's happening and to respond. To make adjustments, shift course, slow down for a moment or accelerate. I am all for the power of team, but often in the early phase of planting we need to be quite discerning who we invite into the dream garden while the soil is still wet and the roots are fragile.

Even though we may be eager to share and gain input from others, in the early days of dream planting, when we are first taking action, there may be a very small handful of people we need to share it with, if any.

For me, the list is very small — my wife Ash, my son Josh, perhaps one or two friends. They are generally people who recognise the power of a young dream in motion, who want the best for me always and can create space in their own dreaming to listen, honour, ask good questions, offer insightful guidance or enthusiasm if requested. We are not looking for flattery but knowing that the first steps toward a dream can be a little awkward and uncertain, and the last thing we want is people pulling at the roots before they have a chance to take hold. We don't want the life of the dream to be squashed or uprooted before it has a chance to start.

Loving insight and inspired reflection, yes please. Micro-analysis and cynicism, no thanks.

∽

When we built our market garden here, we knew we needed help. But again, we wanted to make sure we had the right mix of people to match our vision. And we wanted it to be fun. We chose a combination of two permaculture experts—one seasoned professional and one fresh graduate to balance experienced wisdom with fresh perspective—and a pack of great-vibe teenagers (Josh's best friends) who were ready to get their hands dirty and simply inspired to create something awesome together. Enough knowledge to point in the right direction, with enough freedom to make mistakes, discover the unexpected, laugh and learn along the way. At the end of Day One we had 10 giant log-lined garden beds of tilled and composted soil with mulch on the top, woodchips between sections and a few tiny rows of lettuce lovingly planted to get us started. The group was covered in dirt, straw and smiles. There was no guarantee anything great would happen next, but everyone was quietly infused with the excitement of being part of something magical as it began.

℁

This is the energy I like to have around me in the early phase of a new dream when I first really **plant** it into life.

SPACE, COMPANIONS & THREATS

When we take a seedling from its isolated pot and put it into the ground, as soon as it enters the living soil and mycelia of the garden, we are connecting this seedling to the great network of life. It is no longer alone; it is now part of a greater unfolding story. Likewise, when we start taking real-world action toward our dreams, we enter the wider field of life. In this field there are many other dreams growing that may ultimately influence, weave into or connect with our dream in some way. Where, how and who we include in the early phases of our dream can have a massive impact on its growth.

> *If you want to go fast, go alone.*
> *If you want to go far, go together.*
>
> WEST AFRICAN PROVERB

In the garden and the forest there are certain plants and varieties that grow naturally as companions. When they are planted closely together, each brings a useful or needed element, and they help each other grow.

In life we may also find companion dreams and dreamers (complementary projects and humans) whose presence in our garden help stimulate and support the growth of our dream.

Planting passionfruit vine at the base of lemon tree gives the vine something to grow on and allows us to pick both fruits at the same time. Working alongside someone with complementary skills or working on a dream alongside a related project can help accelerate and deepen the growth of all involved.

My wife Ash will often have multiple paintings going at once and each has a way of informing and supporting the development of the other. My son Josh (a burgeoning music producer) oscillates between focusing on independent tracks he is producing alone and those he creates in collaboration with friends. By running these projects concurrently, it keeps him fresh with ideas flowing to both spaces.

*A viable seed needs favourable conditions, including good light, moisture, warmth and easily accessible soil nutrients, which are generally **not** found under the parent tree.*

KAURI CARE GUIDE
(COMPILED BY STACEY HILL)

We all know the saying that an apple doesn't fall far from the tree, but have you ever noticed that the apples that do fall quite close to the tree don't usually grow into new trees?

Tāne Mahuta, the great kauri, can never grow at the base of its parent tree simply because it needs more sun, light and water than it will receive down there at the base of a giant.

In a similar way, sometimes in the early stages of a dream, we may actually need to create some space between some of the people and environments that know us for who we have been or what we have previously done, in order to be free to grow into who we are committed to becoming.

Even with good intentions, sometimes those who believe they 'know us the best' may unconsciously hold a specific view of what is possible for us which can limit or stifle our growth without us—or even them— knowing it.

This is not to say we need to remove ourselves from the rest of our life, but it's important to realise that dreams bring change. Sometimes when we start listening to the call of our dreams and purpose, it activates that same voice in others, and this can be uncomfortable. Everyone is safe on the veranda simply talking about their dreams until one person picks up a shovel and starts digging in.

There will come a time when your dream garden is thriving and feeding the dreams of many. But sometimes, in the early stages, creating some private space from those who may unknowingly overshadow or threaten the growth of your dream will help you find your footing and build the resilience you will need to go the distance.

TIMING

Some Dream Seeds Arrive Ready to be Planted

There are some seeds (like radishes) we can sprinkle straight into the garden soil, and they will grow almost immediately. They quickly throw roots, sprout forth, and within weeks we are selecting their leaves and bulbs for salads. Likewise, there are some visions that come with such strength and immediacy that our best way to respond is simply to follow them straight into action. If we are ready to move with the wild energy of a dream when it arrives, there is a power born from our "Yes" that allows us to leap forward, build momentum and learn along the way.

A dear friend of mine, author James Twyman, refers to this as, "Chasing the dream down the street." In Jimmy's view, the 'plan' is always going to change, so why waste time over-engineering when you can learn, adapt and grow directly with the pulse of the dream as it emerges.

ஃ

My wife Ash and I knew each other for just two months when we decided to get married. Neither of us had ever even thought the word 'marriage' before we met. But when the impulse arrived it felt like a quiet, clear bolt of lightning that lit up our hearts and the path before us. One month and one day later (by Australian law, this is how long you have to wait) we gathered with family and friends on the beach and planted this dream into the wide-open field of life. Looking back now, nearly 29 years later, I can see how the power of our "Yes", and the deep love within it, literally carried us for the first several years of our marriage. This was long enough to get to know each other a little ☺ and to continue choosing each other in all seasons of the garden of our life together.

*Another friend, sailor/adventurer Jesse Martin, had the impulse at age
17 to sail around the world. Jesse followed the impulse directly, acquired
a small boat, raised enough money and support to begin, and set sail
without ever previously having solo-sailed beyond Port Phillip Bay in
Melbourne. When he left, relatively few people knew about it, and some
of those were placing bets on how quickly he would capsize or return.
A little over a year later—when Jesse arrived back to Australia as the
youngest person ever to solo circumnavigate the globe non-stop and
unassisted—he was greeted by 30,000 people in Sydney Harbour, many
of whom were saying, "We knew you could do it."*

*Jesse said "Yes" to his dream with action and the purity of that "Yes"
carried him through many storms around the world.*

☙

Which of your dreams are sitting on the edge of possibility, waiting not
for more details, research or understanding, but simply for you to begin
with action and chase them down the street?

Some Seeds Require Patient Germination

In contrast to the above examples, there are some seedlings that are more
complex or fragile and may need to stay longer in a smaller, protected
space before being turned loose or planted into life.

In the garden I've learned that some lettuces, herbs and chillies require
certain conditions in order to sprout and grow strong enough to make
the transition into the ground. If we plant them too early, we risk
exposure to the elements, pests and the possibility their root being too
fragile or weak to sustain growth. But we also don't want to wait too
long and let them become rootbound. There is a point at which the soil
in the seedling pot will become lifeless and no longer have nutrients to

feed it. The roots will have nowhere to go, so they will seek escape or start to tangle themselves around each other, ultimately stifling the urge to grow.

Sometimes if we share a dream too early, we risk it being squashed or damaged by the opinions of others who may not yet recognise its potential. This is like scattering fragile seeds into a big garden bed and hoping they survive. But likewise, if we wait too long, holding our dream back in the tangles of our mind, we risk it growing rootbound and losing the life force it was born to express.

We may become fixated on 'getting it right', being realistic or trying to figure it all out before we start, and before we know it, we begin to question the validity of our vision or our ability to pull it off. As the young roots of our dream begin to tangle around themselves in our mind like plant roots in a seedling pot and as they search the bottom for open spaces to escape, we put the seedling back on the shelf in order to 'think it through a little more'. This is a great risk to the dream.

It is important for the dream grower to realise that if this is a genuine dream involving the creation of something *new*, then by its very nature you will never be able to see, imagine or understand all the details before you start. This is what makes it a dream. Because it is beyond what you have seen or experienced before. This doesn't mean we don't do our very best to plan and prepare, but our preparation will never take the place of the simple and magical requirement of stepping into the unknown as we *plant* our dream in the world with action.

Every seed has the right season to grow. We can't grow cucumbers in winter here, but in summer they thrive. Lettuce and leafy greens struggle in the heat of summer, but in winter they pump.

The same is true of our dreams. Each has a season and a timing that is right. We don't want to risk our dream being destroyed by the elements before it has a chance to rise. But equally, and perhaps the greater risk for many, is that we stifle our vision inside the container of our mind until it lacks the energy to grow beyond it. Our job is not to dictate the terms and timing but to listen and respond, even if taking action brings us into the unknown. In most cases, we discover it feels better to be uncomfortable but in motion than rootbound, stagnant or stuck.

PHASES AND DIVERSITY

Planting a dream almost always requires a level of singular focus and devotion, along with the realisation that it may not grow to full fruition overnight.

In the garden, knowing that different crops take different amounts of time to grow and produce different amounts of food, allows us to plan and evolve our efforts through the seasons.

For example, each season we grow certain foods to fulfil our immediate needs (greens, tomatoes, radishes, many above-ground vegetables) knowing that we can begin harvesting in four to six weeks.

While we're doing this, we will also plant more medium-term seedlings we know will be ready in ten to twelve weeks (potatoes, yams, pumpkin, passionfruit) and some fast-growing fruit trees (bananas, papayas) that will fruit in six to nine months.

While the short-term planting gets us eating, the medium-term helps sustain us. The potatoes, pumpkins and bananas take more patience and a little more energy to grow but the yield is stronger, lasts longer and is more substantial. One crop of pumpkins last us all winter, and one rack of bananas makes about 60 smoothies!

Meanwhile, at the top of our field we are also preparing soil and planting longer-term fruit and nut trees which we know will take five to seven years before their first crop. These orchard trees will ultimately yield the greatest long-term abundance, but we would starve if we sat there waiting for them.

Each layer in the garden serves a vital purpose and if we plant these layers consciously, we can harvest and enjoy each garden season in the short term while our longer-term vision grows to full fruition.

⁁⁀

Similar to the layers and phases of growing in the garden, often while we are planting the seeds of our longer-term vision in life, there are simplified expressions of our dream that we can grow in the short-term while building the energy and momentum of the bigger picture.

Take the first step in faith. You don't have to see the whole staircase, just take the first step.

MARIAN WRIGHT EDELMAN

(PARAPHRASING A CONVERSATION WITH MARTIN LUTHER KING JR)

Questions to Consider About the Phases of Your Dream

- What's the simplest expression of your vision?

- What are the immediate, short-term aspects of your dream that could help build energy, momentum and confidence in the journey now? What's one thing you could do today to build, express or experience that energy in action? Think radishes and salad greens … even micro greens!

- What aspects of your dream would you consider to be medium-term?

- What are the bananas and papayas of your dream? What medium-term aspects could you take some to begin growing, knowing they will take three to six months before seeing a result?

- What are the big-picture, bold-vision aspects of your dream?

- What will your life and dream garden look like in five years' time if you continue to ***intend, prepare, plant*** and ***adapt*** your way forward?

Often the longer-term vision is what the initial dream is all about, but the short and medium-term steps help us build clarity and momentum while unlocking aspects of the dream that no amount of thinking and planning ever could. Without taking basic steps to feed and fuel the dream, it will continue to feel out of reach, and we may end up putting way too much pressure on the 'dream orchard' to produce its long-term goal before its time, rather than building patiently and powerfully towards it.

From one avocado seed we might ultimately get 10,000 avocados, plus many seeds for many more trees. One well-written story may reach the hearts and minds of millions, while inspiring hundreds of other stories to be written. Dream cultivation takes patience and a longer-term view (while growing salad along the way), but the outcome is a longer-term gift which may benefit you, your family and many others for generations to come.

Too many dreams never get acted upon because we convince ourselves we can't start until we can go big. Or we spend all our time planning the orchard without growing the simple foods we will need to eat until the avocados and macadamias come in.

Dreams require commitment and they often call for a long-term view, but the place to begin building real energy and real rhythms of the ultimate outcome is almost always right here in the present.

An emerging musician can hold the vision of playing a sold-out stadium concert while giving everything she has in her open mic set at the pub.

A future award-winning director and producer team can work towards box office success by pouring themselves into their roles in a short film production.

You can start being great right now even in small ways. Especially in small ways.

You don't have to wait for the avocados. *Plant* and nurture the avocados, yes. And then get growing the greens!

TRANSITIONING FROM OLD TO NEW

Occasionally saying "Yes" to a dream calls for a radical departure from our current situation (leave one job to begin a new venture, move to a new country to be with a loved one, etc.). But often we can build a natural transition to our dream by allowing the current season of our life to complete itself while simultaneously preparing the soil for the new dreams to grow.

Your dream may have short, medium and long-term steps you can take — often simultaneously. And it's possible you will have multiple dream seeds growing in different phases and different seasons. You may work on a series of short-term projects (salad greens) while you are planning an annual event (bananas) and developing the chapters of a book (avocados). You may need to finish your current job during the day as you cultivate the seeds of an entrepreneurial vision at night. Some old gardens need time to 'go to seed' (more on this later) before the soil can be revitalised and new seeds can grow.

The bottom line is that when we are cultivating a dream—even a long-term vision—we don't need to put our energy on hold. There is always some way, and usually several ways, that we can build, express and harness the energy of our dream.

Some ideas sprout to fruition in the moment. Some bold visions take years to fully mature. You may or may not know your own long-term vision when you start planting seeds — they are just tiny seeds after all!

But the short-term steps you take will help, because they get you into motion, build confidence and momentum — and they feed you along the way.

This is how dream gardens work. And this is why it's important to get *planting*.

THE SIMPLE ACT OF STARTING

In life and creative endeavour, we each come to moments where we are
called to step/leap/dive/***plant*** ourselves into the unknown arena of a new
frontier or dream.

The energy of what is rising within us (a new story, business idea or
life direction), or coming at us (a fresh relationship, bold opportunity
or crisis), means that we can no longer stay where we are. We can plan
and prepare and dance around the edge for a certain amount of time,
but there comes a moment when—for our own sake and the sake of the
dream—we quite simply must begin.

Amidst the pressures of modern life, it's easy to think that the conditions
need to be right in order for us to start. And in truth, every seedling does
have its season … But sometimes the simple act of starting is what makes
the conditions right. From where we stand at the beginning, it may be
impossible to see what lies ahead, but something very powerful happens
when the spark of an idea and the energy of a vision is fed with the
oxygen of committed action. In this moment, the seedling dream
is ***planted***.

The very best news is that no matter where you are, no matter what is
going on or what happens next, the moment you are in right now will
always be your greatest point of power.

To ***plant*** a dream is important work. Our most important work.
I'd go so far as to say that the future of our planet may very well
depend upon it.

REFLECTION

- Which of your seedling dreams are bursting at the seams, ready to go in the ground — or at risk of becoming rootbound if no action is taken, because now is their time?

- Which of your seedling dreams feel most fragile, in need of extra time, space or protective conditions as their roots grow in strength?

- If you could plant ONE idea, project, vision or initiative into your life with action in the next 30 days, what would it be?

- What are one to three simple actions you could take to *plant* that dream into action this week?

ACTION

1. In the next 24 hours, choose at least one tree, plant, herb or vegetable to plant in the ground, somewhere you can keep an eye on it and look after it. If you have no outdoor space to work with, find a friend who does, or create a way to plant and grow indoors.

2. In the next 24 minutes, identify and commit to at least one real action to help plant one dream into your life today. Plant it with love and genuine intent, for the good of all.

3. Set aside a morning this month devoted purely to big-picture thinking and visioning your unique life garden. What are you inspired to grow in the short, medium and long term? What seeds are most alive for you now? What are you committed to growing that may take patience and persistence but will open the field of possibility for many years to come?

6.

WATER
(WITH FAITH AND GRATITUDE)

Love and work are to
people what water and
sunshine are to plants.

JONATHAN HAIDT

Water is the driving force of all nature.

LEONARDO DA VINCI

❧

It's winter here in Australia as I write this. But winter in the subtropics is different than winter in the mountains of Colorado where I grew up. During winter in Colorado, we built ski jumps, not garden beds, in the back yard. Currently my Colorado family's backyard gardens are completely dormant and snow-covered. Here in Australia, the days are cooler, shorter and dryer than in summer, and we grow different things as a result, but the garden still thrives. In summer the cucumbers, tomatoes, chillies, zucchini, pumpkin and many varieties of fruit trees absolutely pump. In winter, we couldn't grow a cucumber if we wanted to (and I wanted to!), but the Asian greens, lettuce, rocket, arugula, broccoli, cauliflower, snow peas and radishes are growing faster than we can eat and share them.

By the time I finished writing the last chapter I was so fired up about planting, and felt such a renewed sense of responsibility to the winter seedlings we've been propagating, that I spent the better part of two days putting everything possible into the ground — including many of the listed winter veggies and about 15 young trees and native flowering bushes we have been preparing in pots.

I was excited to give these potted life forms the space and ground to grow, and felt proud of myself for unleashing their true potential by planting them into the ground. I was traveling for a few days the following week, so it was several days before I had a chance to properly check up on my freshly planted seedlings. To my surprise there had been very little growth, and in fact a few of them looked like they had actually shrunk!

What happened?

I had nurtured these little seedlings until they were bursting forth ready to be planted … I had dug them in with care and good wishes, but here they were, smaller and weaker than they had been in their little pots.

A closer look revealed that yes, they did have access to vastly more space and nutrients of the garden, but they were also way more exposed to the elements than they had been in the nursery. A couple days of dry wind while I was away, and these little guys were really feeling it.

As I ran for the hose and water bucket, I was reminded how fragile these phases of transition can be — for a seedling and a dream.

When we commit to the planting, this is a critically important step as it allows for the full realisation of potential, but this is not the end of the journey. It is really just another beginning.

Once the seedlings are in the ground, their access to the nutrients required to fulfil their potential is instantly multiplied, but so are the risks they face. In many cases, they cannot make the journey alone. Especially in the beginning. They need ample amounts—sometimes extra amounts—of water, protection and light.

There is a key step in the planting phase often referred to as 'watering in', where we take the time to soak the new seedling with more water than it would normally need, before putting it into the ground. This allows the little roots to fully hydrate and loosen off from their compacted position in the seedling pot, and it acts as a sort of turbo boost for its transition into the garden.

I had watered in this batch of seedlings when I planted them and thought my job was done. But the dry winds of winter reminded me that every season and seed is different. Our job is not to decide what they need, but to notice, observe and be dynamic in our willingness to take action in response.

Depending on the season, soil conditions, weather and what else is growing around them, some seedlings will grow quickly from here without much further help. Some will take their time to settle in and require extra support and a watchful eye to make sure they are receiving all the light, water and protection they need to navigate their way up amidst the rest of the garden.

It's easy to be grateful for the plant or tree once it is fully bearing fruit, but what I've realised is that the harvest is not the most important time for our gratitude, belief and attention. It is here in these early days as the tender roots weave their way into the soil and the tiny leaves and shoots are reaching up. Much like the early days of a dream, now is when they need our support, trust and gratitude the most.

This week I recommitted myself to the daily practice of watering and spending time checking in on the new seedlings, respecting and responding to the fragile process of transition they are moving through.

I'm not putting pressure on them to grow faster than they are capable. I'm not disturbing them or digging them up to check on their roots. I'm simply watering them with gratitude for the journey they are making, exposing them to sunlight, providing the most supportive conditions possible and trusting nature to do the rest.

໑

MEETING NATURE'S PACE

When we first plant a dream into action, depending on the size and scale of the dream, it may or may not grow at the pace we expect. Sometimes it's slower, sometimes faster. Certain dreams require intensive focus right up front, while others will find a slower, steady pace of momentum over time. Like our current garden crop of lettuce and radishes—that seem to sprout as soon as we plant them—the dream may grow faster than we can eat it. Or, like the young kauri tree, there may be months or even years between when we *plant* our seedling dream and when we see real outward evidence of growth.

Often by the time we *plant* a dream, we have already been thinking about it for a while. We have a vision of our ultimate outcome, we've brainstormed ideas, we've mapped out a plan, we've talked to close allies and it all feels quite real — even before we've taken any real steps. Because of this, we may naturally expect that the moment we *plant* the dream it will start bearing fruit.

And sometimes it does. In fact, sometimes a dream is so ready to grow that as soon as we speak it into the ether it seems to start manifesting around us. Other times, the pace and direction of growth is different than we had planned for or ever could have imagined.

Often, like in the garden, there can be a lag between our first steps on the outside and the dream's first reflections back to us as progress. Occasionally, our first steps forward actually feel like a leap backwards!

If your dream is to get into the best physical shape of your life but you haven't exercised for years, your first few workouts might feel humbling, awkward and even painful! Your vision is clear and you are fully committed, but as you start working out every day, the chances are high that before you experience any of the outward benefits of being fit, you will first experience the gaps in your fitness and the discomfort of sore muscles (as they break down and learn to grow stronger than before). This is all part of the dream journey, but at first it may just feel difficult.

In this time gap, our tendency can be to doubt the dream or our readiness for it. But this is not the time to dig up the dream by its roots. This is not the time to question its validity or try to force our agenda upon it. We don't want to quit the gym just because we feel worse on

Day Three than we did on Day One. Our job is to trust the process, continue digging in to give the dream all the energy and water it needs … and to give thanks for these early rhythms of growth (inside or out).

FAITH AND GRATITUDE

The time to be grateful for the dream is not when it's finished and complete. It's now, when it is young and just beginning to grow. These early days when the progress is not visible, when the momentum is not strong, when the opinions of others may not be in our favour — this is when our dream needs our positive energy and belief the most.

We don't need to flood our dream with unwarranted accolades, but if we starve the dream of our encouragement until it is fully grown, it will likely never reach its full potential. In the same way that seedlings in our garden need *water* and light to grow, dreams that have a been planted into our life, need consistent action coupled with faith and gratitude to help build strength to navigate the journey.

Faith is not wishful thinking. It's not guessing or hoping. Faith comes from knowing that we have done everything we can each day to play our part, combined with an inner knowing that we are not the only force at play. The great natural rhythms of life play their part, and some would say that the heartbeat of the dream itself has a role to play. Faith comes from a sense of inner knowing that our deep intent and daily actions will meet the greater forces of life — and this convergence will bring ideas and vision into form.

In the garden and in life, clear intent and committed action are both required, but sometimes our desire for something to develop can cause us to put unnatural pressure on the situation or force actions that run the risk of pushing away or constricting the growth. Our role as growers of dreams is to bring our part in full to the mission, while also trusting Life to guide, respond and help set the pace.

Our faith may start small like a seedling but it too must grow over time — until we are so clear and strong in our connection and commitment to the pulse of our dream that we can withstand any of the forces that challenge us en route to our dream's full realisation.

Gratitude for the seemingly insignificant—a seed—
this plants the giant miracle.

ANN VOSKAMP

THE POWER OF PRACTICE: THE WATERING CAN OF DREAMS

When we witness professional athletes, artists and other public figures performing their dream at its peak, we often see the finished picture and end result (the Olympic-winning run, the award-winning performance), but we rarely see the consistent, disciplined journey that got them there. We don't see the quiet days of cultivation, the showing up when they are exhausted or resistant, the struggles and vulnerability, the watering, the faith and belief.

In the same way that the garden responds to consistent rhythms of sun and rain, so do our dreams to the daily practices we build to honour, protect and nourish them.

Our role during the early phase of our dream's growth is to hold a very clear vision for the ultimate outcome of our seedling, while simultaneously being completely present, accepting and responsive to it, exactly where it is. To watch it, to listen to it, to hold it loosely and create the environment that will most support it to grow to the next level.

Like a musical instrument with fresh strings, we are tuning it and *tuning in* to it simultaneously. We play a few notes, listen intently, and tune a little more.

Like parents of a child who is just learning to crawl, we aren't pressuring this child to walk too soon. We are down there on the ground with them, loving this moment right where we are, while knowing that this is just the very beginning of an epic journey towards walking, running, leaping and dreaming.

Often during the dream-growing journey, we will find there is a gap between our ultimate vision and the current reality of our dream. Between where we are and where we ultimately aspire and commit to being. This does not mean something is wrong. This simply means we are on the path. And if the path before us is not entirely clear and visible, this also does not mean something is wrong. In many cases this simply means we are moving toward something *new* — beyond where we have been previously.

The very nature of moving into the new is that we will be leaving behind aspects of ourselves and the road we have walked so far as we enter unknown territory. This can bring up all sorts of feelings of anxiousness and uncertainty, but again it does not mean that something is wrong. It simply means we are stepping from the known elements of our past experience into the calling of our dream.

Consider a road trip from your home to the other side of a mountain range. As soon as you leave the comfort of your place of departure, you will be aware of the gap between where you started and your ultimate destination. This gap does not mean you are not committed or that the journey is not worth taking. It's simply an invitation to align your coordinates then settle in and focus your attention on the present moment unfolding on the winding road beneath you. In fact, once you know where you are going, you can't get there any faster by focusing on the end.

The only way to reach your ultimate destination is by bringing your energy and attention to the moment you are in.

The opportunity for the dreamer is to learn to hold both the ultimate outcome and this moment on the journey in our hands at the same time. To be 100 per cent committed to our vision *and* to trust it enough that we allow ourselves to be completely present right here — honouring and responding to what is, creating space for what's ready to emerge.

The dream is our inner compass, but we can't focus on the road while our eyes are fixated on the map. We must trust enough in the bigger picture unfolding that we allow ourselves to be where we are, hands on the wheel, feeling the road, enjoying the scenery as it passes.

Our greatest point of power is always in the present. Even if we are trying to create something beyond our current reality.

If you are a speaker and have a vision of speaking live to 10,000 people but the first time you hold a talk there are only 10 in the room, you don't abandon the vision or pull up the dream by its roots. You show up for those 10 people like they are the most important 10 people in the world, and you build the energy and connection so strongly that when you eventually do have an amphitheatre of 10,000, each person feels as though you are speaking directly to them in a small group of 10! If you are a writer finishing your first book, your dream may be for this book to be a global bestseller, but the only way there is to refine the sentence right in front of you. If you are a skier with your sights on Olympic gold in four years' time, that dream may be the compass that gets you out of bed in the morning, but the progress needed to reach your ultimate outcome will only come from being on the mountain, pouring love and intention into each turn, each breath, one run at a time.

Embody the essence of your ultimate vision (your dream) while being 100 per cent present with—and grateful for—the moment you are in.

BUILDING A PRACTICE IN SERVICE OF YOUR DREAM

Energy flows where attention goes.

HAWAIIAN KAHUNA PRECEPT

One of the most powerful ways of creating both trust and momentum is by cultivating a daily practice in service of what you are committed to.

Defined by the Cambridge dictionary as, "the act of doing something regularly or repeatedly to improve your skill at doing it," our practice is the regular, focused effort or attention we give to our dream. It's the simple things we do day to day that build energy, momentum and confidence over time.

The dream-building practice is about establishing daily rhythms of focused intent and action in service of our dream. It's about learning to embrace the plateaus between growth spurts as an opportunity to consolidate learning, notice the small wins and give oxygen to the breakthroughs. The dream-building practice is about being so immersed in the journey that we actually stop keeping score, while at the same time not missing an opportunity to celebrate a goal scored, acknowledge effort and experience the joy of measured growth over time.

Building a practice is something we can do both internally (**water** the roots) and externally (**water** the leaves), recognising that growth happens on multiple levels. Sometimes the dream needs more expanded thought, sometimes it simply needs more action.

The practice is aimed at giving the dream what it needs each day without forcing it to grow too quickly or produce fruit to soon. If we feed it too aggressively, we can burn the roots. Too much water and they may rot. Too much pressure in the hose can bend or break branches. We need to 'regulate the pressure' with what we feed our garden, and this applies also to our dreams. Too much pressure to produce an outcome too soon can burn us out. Not enough intensity or focus and the dream may starve or go stagnant.

When I build a daily practice toward a dream—or any area of desired growth—I'm always considering two key aspects:

- ***The Outer Practice*** — What is the 'physical goal' or 'outward expression' of my dream. How can I build the skills, capabilities or simple steps toward that outcome today?

- ***The Inner Practice*** — What is the 'feeling-based' outcome of my dream or vision? How can I cultivate that feeling on the inside on a daily basis?

The Outer Practice often seems like the obvious place to start. Measurable results and action are what's needed, so the outer focus is where our attention often goes. And rightfully so. If I want to be a better surfer, I need spend more time catching waves. I need to eat well, rise early, stretch, move, study the ocean, paddle out, paddle hard, pay attention and surf — as much as possible. If I want to write a book, I need to show up, clear my space, charge the laptop, build the outline, block the time and write — every day.

The Outer Practice is like watering the leaves and branches of our dream. It's the routine external activities that are needed without question, to make progress, acquire skills, gain fluency in the area we are committed to growing.

But outward action is not the only thing that's needed to grow the dream. In fact, in most cases, the outer actions we take are a by-product or reflection of our inner sense of alignment and intention. The two work together to create the overall impact of our movement towards a dream.

As much as we need focused external rhythms aligned with our dream, we also need clear internal rhythms to support its growth, to expand our visions and also to know when enough is enough. We need to **water** the leaves and shoots, but we also need to **water** the roots of the dream. These exist inside the thoughts, feelings and beliefs we have about ourselves, our capabilities and what we are moving towards.

In concept, most people recognise the connection between our inner state (thoughts, feelings, beliefs) and our external outcome. But we don't always consider, in a practical sense, how we actually build a positive, cohesive connection between these two forces in the direction of our intended outcome.

YOUR FEELING-BASED OUTCOME

One of the ways we do this is by taking time to clarify and build focused energy of intent around what I refer to as a 'feeling-based outcome'. What is the end-result feeling of our goal or effort? How do we want to *feel* once we have achieved or accomplished the thing that we are setting out to do?

The importance of being connected with our feeling-based outcome (along with our external goal) is that the path doesn't always unfold exactly as we plan it to, and the dream doesn't always look exactly like we envisioned it to from the beginning.

My Olympic dream as an athlete looked very different when it began materialising in my role as a coach, but the essence of the experience—the feeling of reaching the pinnacle of this sport in a major global event—was still deeply aligned with my dream. It was just expressing itself in a different way. In my case, the act of channelling the energy of my individual dream into supporting and igniting the dreams of others was actually a chance to expand the original feeling and ultimately play a bigger game.

If I had been fixated on my mental picture of reaching the Olympics as an athlete, I may have continued pushing and injuring my body to the point of no return, and completely missed seeing the dream materialise in a different form.

When we are connected to the feeling-based outcome of a dream we can take empowered actions in the outside world and recognise the progress we are making, even if the form does not match our initial mental picture. With the end-result feeling as our inner compass, we can move very powerfully in the direction of the dream while remaining open to how it evolves.

This is particularly helpful when we are building energy towards a dream or vision that is beyond what we may have created or experienced in the past. If it is authentically a new dream, we may not actually know what it's going to look like when we achieve it. But if we can get clear about what it's going to *feel* like, then this feeling becomes a deep compass that not only guides our actions in a very natural way, it also gives us a clear place to start!

The less empowering alternative is that we may start the dream journey with an inner dialogue that says, "Once I've achieved X, then I will feel Y", "Once I've won the gold medal, then I will feel a sense of achievement", "Once I've been promoted to manager, then I will feel valued and respected as a leader", or "Once I receive that award or accolade, then I will feel confident in what I'm doing."

In my experience, the 'Once X, then Y' equation almost never works out.

When how we feel on the inside is dictated purely by what happens on the outside, we are now at the effect of the world around us. This is a precarious place to be as a dreamer. Particularly if what we want to achieve is pioneering or in some way new to the world.

BUILDING THE INNER DREAM

Especially in these early phases of the dream, we need to build a sense of deep inner self-reliance, rather than looking for validation on the outside to fuel our steps. If we can get a clear sense for how we want to feel at the end, then we have a golden key. This same feeling is what we need to start bringing to the beginning.

The way I like to think about it is: whatever we want to *get out of the dream,* we need to learn to *bring to the dream.*

Here's a simple example how an Inner Practice and feeling-based intent has impacted my dream of becoming a better surfer.

ೞ

When I first migrated from the mountains of Colorado to the ocean of Australia and started learning to surf, I assumed it would be a simple transfer of mountain skills to sea. And while the actual surfing part did feel quite natural, just about everything else leading up to the standing-on-the-wave part was new and quite humbling to say the least. Tides, currents, swell direction, wind direction, how to paddle, how to get out, how to get back in, how to be in the right spot at the right time, moving at the right speed to match the pace of a rolling wall of water that has travelled thousands of miles to arrive here as a wave (and how to do all this without crashing into someone else) … this was all new territory.

I had always been a hard worker, so I figured if I just showed up every day and paddled out, sooner or later (hopefully sooner) I would be riding waves with the same level of confidence that I had learned to ride mountains.

If you have ever been to a popular surf spot early in the morning, you will be familiar with the visible urgency surfers have to get in the water once they arrive. Because so many conditions must come together to make waves great for surfing, when it's 'on' there's a sense of immediacy that causes grown adults to abandon formalities and sprint along the beach like children just to get to the water a few seconds quicker.

*It was strange to witness this when I first arrived at the sport, but as soon as I caught my first wave, I instantly experienced the same sense of visceral magnetism. Arrive. Glance to the water. Avoid tripping while throwing on wetsuit. Grab board. Wax board (if necessary).
Run. Paddle. Begin!*

This was a great approach in the beginning because it 'got me out there'. But over time, I noticed that—even though I appeared to be doing what others were—my surfing performance was highly inconsistent and haphazard. Some days, I caught 10 waves in 30 minutes and felt at one with the Universe. Other days, I got stuck on the 'inside' (couldn't get out past the breaking waves) or drifted waveless out to sea. Strangely, this phenomenon wasn't condition specific. Some of my best surfs happened in challenging, stormy conditions, and some of my biggest frustrations were on glassy, offshore days when everyone else seemed to be catching the waves of their lives.

Initially, I put this down to the painful learning curve of surfing combined with some cosmic punishment for starting later in life. Then one day, while following my normal sprinting protocol to the ocean, something stopped me at the water's edge that would change my surfing forever.

The waves looked awesome and surfers were pouring into the water, frothing to get out to the line-up as fast as possible. But just for a moment, I stopped.

I stopped with the thought that maybe the reason I was having such mixed results was that I was relying completely on external forces—many of which I didn't fully understand—to dictate the outcome of my session. I was trying my hardest and hoping for the best, but I was missing one simple ingredient: a clearly felt intention for the experience I wanted to create.

I was asking the ocean to send me waves, but I wasn't actually taking time to tune in with myself, with the elements themselves or with the experience that was about to happen. I was rushing into the water like a violinist arriving late to the orchestra, hoping I could play my note right at the crescendo without even taking time to tune up.

Because the ocean is always changing and I was learning something new, it was not easy for me to visualise riding a perfect wave. But what I could imagine was how I would feel on the other side of riding such a wave. I could imagine myself stepping from the water, excitedly exhausted, alive and inspired — feelings I knew from many experiences in nature. I could feel gratitude in my body for having had a beautiful session. I could imagine being dripping wet with a contented smile, walking back up the beach knowing that I had experienced something new and exciting — perhaps a 'wave of my life' moment. I didn't know exactly what this would look like, but I could conjure in my mind and body what it would feel like. As I let myself feel this feeling for just a few seconds at the water's edge, I noticed a natural rising of calm, inspired energy. I felt connected. I started smiling, somehow already content with the surf I hadn't even had yet. I took a few deep breaths and let the feeling sink in. When my whole body was saturated with this energy, I let it all go and stepped into the water with that feeling as my compass.

I paddled into the wave zone amidst a pack of other surfers, most of whom were technically more advanced than me. After about 30 seconds, a wave rose to a peak right in front of me. I turned, paddled onto it and soared down the line! Wow — that was quick! I paddled back out and within a minute, just as I was catching my breath, another wave seemed to weave its way right through the pack to me. My eyes widened. I turned, paddled and caught that one too — all the way to the sand. I continued the session like this for the next 45 minutes until I'd caught more waves than I could count, with a more than a few 'wave of my life' moments! When I finally left the water and returned to my starting place on the beach, it struck me that the same feeling I had set as my compass before I entered the water was now flooding my whole being.

This simple practice of pausing for a moment to feel the feeling of my end-result outcome transformed my surfing experience from that session to this very day, many years later.

☙

The ocean of life (and the garden of dreams) is always changing and evolving. We cannot predict or control how she will move moment to moment, but we can set a compass on the inside that lines us up with the overall feeling of the experience we are committed to creating. Rather than waiting for the external world to dish up our experience in order to validate our 'hopes', we can start from the other side, by clearly anchoring the end-result feeling, and let that feeling guide, drive and shape our experience.

When I paddle out into the water with a genuine feeling of gratitude for the experience that I'm about to have, even though I can't foresee the exact details, two fundamental things happen:

1. I become far less reliant on the external forces or physical 'outcome' to satisfy how I feel about the experience. I am now bringing the positive energy *to* the experience that I had previously hoped to take *from* the experience.

2. Because of this, I become naturally aligned with the external forces (in this case, the ocean) and moment-to-moment decisions that are in-tune with the feelings and experience I am committed to creating.

In the same way that playing a note on one guitar causes the same string of another instrument to vibrate, when I paddle out into the ocean playing a note of gratitude and inspired connection, I come into alignment with experiences that resonate with that feeling. Just like two instruments playing together, the shared note between me and the ocean starts to grow and together we move. Without over-thinking it, I find myself responding to subtle impulses to paddle a little bit to the left or right, move out a bit deeper, let this wave pass and wait for the next, etc. I become less reactive to what others are doing and suddenly I find myself in the right place at the right time to meet a wave that has travelled thousands of miles across the ocean to rise to a peak with me! I paddle with commitment, but not desperation. I'm inspired beyond words, but not surprised. My job here is to clearly embody the feeling I'm committed to creating in the experience (by feeling it). The ocean's job is to reflect that feeling back to me. This is the seed that was planted while standing at the shore, and here she is rising to meet me. *Whooooosh!* And we soar down the breaking wave together.

In surfing, this feeling-based outcome often manifests in the form of super-fun waves to surf, but sometimes it takes different forms — a pod of dolphins swimming past and pausing to connect, a simple break in the clouds for a ray of sun to blast through, a moment of total stillness in the pouring rain. The amazing thing is, if I am guided by the *feeling*, and I remain open to what form it takes, life *always* delivers — often in ways we never could have imagined!

In surfing, dream building and life, building a daily 'practice' in service of our mission is one of the keys to creating energetic momentum and unleashing the limitless potential that exists within each moment. Our job is to do the simple things day-to-day that help us be our very best. Part of this preparation is found in the external actions we take each day — the physical fitness for our dream. And an equal part is found in the way that we line ourselves up on the inside with the feeling of the experience we are committed to creating. Not waiting until the work is done to give ourselves permission to feel good. But recognising that feeling good is not the end result but a precursor and pathfinder to the dream.

This is how we **water** the roots to grow our dream strong and deep from the inside.

> # Vision without action is merely a dream. Action without vision just passes the time. Vision with action can change the world.
>
> JOEL A. BARKER

THE OUTER AND THE INNER

The principles of practice-building can (and should) be applied to any arca of life or creative endeavour in which we are committed to being our best. In my work as a coach and facilitator, my Outer Practices tend to be related directly to my business and involve specific disciplines that help me feel centred when I'm busy. They include setting and balancing my schedule prior to each week (including loading certain days with certain types of work and leaving open spaces for reflection between meetings), being pro-active in my communication (including formal, planned and spontaneous outreach) and taking time to prepare (including blocking out sections of my week to think and design workshops).

My Inner Practices are a little different. Sometimes they relate directly to my business, but are more often built around key activities that have no obvious link to the work, but set me up 'on the inside' to feel centred, aligned and inspired in whatever I am doing. Rising early, writing in my journal, surfing, ice baths, saunas, time in the garden, time with bees, time with God, breathing, walking amidst trees, playing music with Ash, listening to music with Josh … These are all items on a menu of 'lifeforce-building' activities that I know have a massive positive impact on my state of *being*, my perspective and the energy of my approach in everything I need to *do* — including showing up powerfully with and for my clients as a coach.

In the beginning, building discipline around an Outer or Inner Practice can be challenging. It takes time, deliberate action and may disrupt our previous 'normal' way of doing things. This is part of the journey. In fact, it should be a disruption. Waking up an hour earlier to move, write in your journal or have an ice bath isn't convenient. Some days it may feel painful or impossible to get out of bed. But each day we pull back the covers and rise, we build a new layer of energy and momentum for our dream.

We are cultivating a new type of fitness, which involves breaking down and building up, contracting, breathing and expanding into the new.

It's worth noting that if we aren't consciously building practices toward what we want to create, we may be unconsciously feeding habits and practices that are keeping us in a holding pattern, or in some cases moving us further away from our dream. Whatever we repeatedly give focus to grows, so part of the process of developing a practice is about becoming more deliberate and disciplined about what we choose to focus our thoughts, words, actions and energy on.

When you look at the daily patterns of activity in your life, what habits are serving and building momentum towards your dream? What are you currently 'practising' (in thought, word or deed) that could be keeping your dream at bay?

Over time, our practices not only cultivate the energy and resilience we need to navigate the dreamscape, they serve as a tuning fork to help us know where we are and what is needed next. In sport, the more fit our body and mind become, the more our body and mind speak to us, sending us signals and feedback along the way. In life and dream building, our practices do the same. They tune us in to internal and external cues of our mission and bring clarity and confidence to take the next step.

As we ***water*** our dream with daily practice (inside and out), feed it with gratitude for where it is now and faith in all it is becoming, we weave a rhythm of connection between the pulse of our dream and forces of nature conspiring to bring it to full fruition.

REFLECTION

- When you imagine your dream in full, thriving fruition, how do you imagine that you will *feel*? What is the 'end-result feeling' of your dream?

- What is a simple action you could take on a daily basis as a 'practice' (inside or out) to build the energy of your dream?

- How can you create that feeling in your mind, heart, body and actions today?

ACTION

1. Whatever new plants or young trees you now have growing in your garden (or house), make a special effort to notice what they need this week (more water, more light, more shade, more space) and give it to them — not with an expectation for them to 'perform' or give you more of something in return, but with simple gratitude for where they are on their journey and what they may one day become.

2. Whatever new dream, idea or vision you are currently working on, take a few minutes to write down all the things you are already grateful about with this dream. What do you love about it, including how it is challenging you? Take some time to ***water*** your dream today with gratitude for what it already is and faith for all that it is becoming.

3. Commit to building (or expanding) a daily 'practice' in service of your dream for the next 30 days:

    *   On the Outside: 1–2 simple disciplines and activities that—if applied daily for the next month—will help you organise, clarify and build external momentum for your dream. What simple action could you give your dream on daily basis to help it grow?

    *   On the Inside: 1–2 simple disciplines or activities that—if applied daily for the next month—will help you build the energy, centredness and inspiration you need to be your very best.

7.

WEEDS
(WILL RISE ... AND THEY'RE NOT ALL WEEDS!)

Weeds are flowers, too, once you get to know them.

A. A. MILNE

Since we started growing food in this rich-soiled region, probably the only thing that has rivalled our appreciation for how quickly the seedlings we plant grow to fruition, is our astonishment for how rapidly weeds, wild grasses and competitive vines find their way into the soil and thrive as well. While the tender roots and early growth of our seedlings often hang in the fragile balance of the elements (and our ability to protect them), their wild plant counterparts seem to arrive deeply rooted and (f!#king) resilient from the start.

In recent years, thankfully we've discovered that many of the plants that the world calls weeds actually play important roles in restoring the balance of the soil while having highly medicinal qualities for our bodies. Conversely, we've also discovered that some vegetables we consciously plant in the garden can actually have a negative or overbearing impact on the garden—and our bodies—if we're not watchful.

As with the garden of our dreams, there are the seeds which we plant on purpose, and there are the forces in life that emerge and grow around them — some of which help inspire our next steps, some of which distract or pull away our energy. With gardens and dreams, certain weeds grow in plain view, are easy to spot and address, while others emerge more subtly from under the surface, draining the nutrients of our creative soil without us being aware. Strangely enough, some of our most seemingly disruptive weeds may ultimately become our greatest allies.

☙

The following are a few things we're discovering about **weeds** that might help harness the gifts these wild forces bring to both our garden and dreams in life.

WHEN RAIN FALLS, EVERYTHING GROWS

Nature does not discriminate. When rain falls and sun shines on fertile soil, dormant seeds, whose season has come, will wake up and begin to rise. The roots and shoots of our young seedlings take hold and begin to grow towards fruition, and so will whatever else is in the soil around them — including what the world refers to as **weeds**.

Some seeds and roots of wild plants rest in the soil for months or years before they are activated by a new growth cycle. Others are blown there by the breeze, dropped there by birds or migrate into the garden from other places, drawn in by the fertility of the soil. Preparing the garden bed, as discussed earlier, can certainly help slow the invasion. But as soon as rain and sun hit our soil, we all begin to see what else is waiting in there, ready to grow.

In life, some of the most challenging forms of **weeds** we carry are the thoughts, core beliefs and past experiences that subconsciously influence our day-to-day activities. Much like the interwoven root system of plants below the surface, each of us have an entire ecosystem of perceptions and conditioning patterns that weave together just below the surface of our actions, sending messages about what is and isn't possible, what we are and aren't capable of, worthy of, ready for.

Often when we start moving in the direction of a new idea or dream, this movement activates some of these deeper, dormant inklings to stir inside of us. Similar to the weeds rising in our early garden, these forces—including doubts, fears, distraction and self-judgement—can be vigorous, and often seem to rise faster than the dreams themselves.

Some subconscious patterns are helpful and can become fuel for our growth; some are disruptive and may threaten to climb over the top of our seedling dream before we even know they are there.

Here's an example of how this can work…

*An artist has a clear vision one evening for an inspired new painting
and goes to sleep excited to start painting in the morning. She chooses
the canvas (it's a big one, worthy of this bold vision) and sets up the
space imagining her first strokes with the brush. But it's getting a
little late to start something new, so she decides to sleep on the idea
and get started in the next day.*

*She sleeps and dreams and by the time she wakes, brews her coffee
and enters the studio, the vision is still there but it is now coupled
with sleepiness, a few distracting thoughts and a slight sense of doubt
about her ability to translate that vision into reality. She's not sure
exactly where to start on the canvas, so she decides to wait for a
few hours, take care of some other daily tasks, let the starting place
percolate, and begin painting in the evening.*

*Night-time comes, along with some family responsibilities and a few
unexpected requests from others, so she shifts her plan to kick off fresh
the following morning undistracted.*

*By sunrise of Day Two, the clarity of the vision has begun to fade
a little and the feeling of excitement that came with the initial
idea now feels a bit flat — surrounded by a variety of little doubts,
uncertainty and even some memories about other painting ideas that
never got finished.*

*By Day Three she can still see the vision, but her quiet rumination
is now growing into guilt and self-judgement for not yet starting.
These thoughts, ideas and memories now seem to be spiralling with
intensity, growing faster and stronger around the fragile edges of her
painting idea.*

On Day Four she is distracted by a friend who needs her help to complete an exhibition she's been planning.

By Day Five the initial vision for her new, inspired painting feels lost in a field of everything else growing around it. She starts thinking maybe it wasn't such a good idea anyway and decides to wait for the next bolt of lightning to help clarify what painting she should really be working on, as she starts second guessing if she should even be painting at all …

Much like the ***weeds*** that grow in our garden, dormant thoughts and energies can have a way of rising with more strength and velocity than our young seedling dreams. If we are unaware of this phenomenon, the weeds of our dreams may quickly overwhelm or undermine our pursuit. But if we are watchful, curious and discerning, we will learn how to deal with and work with these rising forces for the greater good of our dream and the garden. Ultimately, we will discover that many rising weeds—even the ones with thorns—often come with a gift.

Weed (noun):
A plant that is not valued where it is growing and is usually of vigorous growth.

MERRIAM-WEBSTER DICTIONARY

NOT ALL WEEDS ARE WEEDS

In a conversation with David Holmgren, one of the pioneering founders of permaculture, he estimated that approximately 70 per cent of the plants we identify as *weeds* in our gardens actually have high nutritious value for our bodies and the soil — often far more nutritional beneficial than the food we are consciously trying to grow.

Even though some weeds and wild plants may appear to compete with the garden seedlings, in many cases they would not be growing there if they did not serve a purpose. Dandelions, for example, are often perceived as a problem and distraction from the 'real' garden or lawn we're trying to grow, while in fact they are one of the most diversely beneficial and nutrient-dense plants available to humans and soil.

Since ancient times in China, Rome and Greece, the dandelion plant (flower, stem, leaves and root) has been used for a wide range of medicinal purposes, ranging from headache relief and improved vision to depression alleviation, immune system boosting, brain function, liver function and cholesterol balancing — to name a few! Meanwhile, the tap roots of the plant help to loosen compacted soil (have you noticed the way dandelions will even grow through the crack of a sidewalk?) and draw much-needed nutrients from deep beneath the surface to where they can be accessed by other plants. As one of the first plants to flower each spring, they attract beneficial pollinators and provide both pollen and nectar for bees. All hail the dandelion!

Wild plants like dandelions are strong because they have evolved over many thousands of years to find a way to grow and perpetuate life in all conditions. They are strong because they have needed to be in order to survive. They can be vigorous and highly strategic in their growing patterns, and often a lot harder to pull out and remove than the tender roots of our seedlings.

They may or may not have a long-term place in our garden, but their strength and dynamic growing habits often serve a purpose and, at very least, should be respected and learned from. With the dandelion, once it has done its work of fixing nitrogen in the soil for the next generation of plants and grasses to thrive, in most cases it will slowly send its seeds downwind to the next field that needs to be replenished. And then it will move on.

WHERE ARE YOUR DANDELIONS?

If you see a dandelion as a weed, you'll spray it. If you see it as a flower, you'll draw it close, turn it this way and that, and become lost in the colossal burst of slender golden petals that spew sunshine into the darkest of souls. And so, how many things have we sprayed that could have illuminated our souls if we would have let them be more than what we let them be?

CRAIG D. LOUNSBROUGH

It's powerful to consider that even though the dandelions are an incredible force for good in the garden, because they weren't part of the 'plan', our first response is often to try getting rid of them. Is it possible that this knee-jerk reaction also applies to other areas of life where things we don't consciously plan for start growing more powerfully than our initial goal?

The opportunity for the grower (of gardens and dreams) is to look first with great curiosity to understand why the wild plant has arrived, so we know what purpose it may be playing in the overall cycle of life and the journey towards realising our dream.

If we have been clear of ***intent***, we have ***prepared*** the soil of our life
and taken time to ***plant*** and ***water*** our dream, we can be sure that
as our dream begins to grow, so will other things around it — fresh
impulses and ideas, new relationships and influences. If we can remain
simultaneously grounded in our commitment to our dream *and* open to
what emerges along the way, we may find complementary forces rising
and weaving into our dream that we never could have imagined.

The first thing to consider when addressing ***weeds*** (in garden or life), is
to recognise that just because you didn't plan or plant it, it may still have
a reason for being there. And some of the things we actually try to block
from growing may actually be our greatest allies if we allow them to rise
and reveal their gifts.

*It's Day Six for the artist, and the detailed vision for her inspired
painting now feels like a distant memory, completely overgrown by
the doubts in her mind and the distractions of life. She walks into her
studio to collect something and feels an instant ache in her gut —
the ache of tangled, stuck creative energy now turning in on itself.
She feels far from her dream and angry at herself for procrastinating.*

*In her anger, she picks up a paintbrush, dips it into paint and throws
it against the canvas, splattering colour across the empty space.
She grabs another one and starts sweeping it across the canvas with
no thought whatsoever. Back and forth, up and down — big, wild,
sweeping movements. Now with her hands, dipping them into the
paint and running them recklessly across the white. Her whole body is
moving now, she's talking and yelling at the canvas. Releasing all the
frustration and angst of her previous days.*

*This does not feel like art. This is nothing like her 'plan', but the
energy is moving and with each wild stroke, it feels good. Freeing.*

She opens her movement across the entire canvas, covering it completely with a myriad of colours.

Out of breath, she drops to the floor, covered in paint, somewhere between surrender, laughter and tears. Half-afraid to look, she glances up to her canvas — raw, splattered and dripping with all the emotions of her outburst. She thinks of all the other artists that must have versions of this feeling as they approach their canvas with the pressure to be good enough, to be right, to create 'art' and beauty …

As her breath slows and deepens, her eyes focus lightly on the colours and lines and begin to distinguish a shape which somehow resembles the face of a woman in the middle of the canvas. Looking closer she sees other details begin to naturally reveal themselves.

She picks up a brush and begins to lightly work with the natural shapes and distinguish them … the hair, the eyes. It's abstract and unexpected, but there is feeling there, an aliveness. A raw beauty which is now informing her with each stroke of the brush. Instead of trying to 'make' her painting look like something, this canvas is drawing her in, guiding her eyes and movement, revealing itself gently for her to unfold.

The struggle and constraint of previous days falls away and, in this moment, she feels embraced by the art of life and discovers a whole new way of creating!

WORKING WITH THE WEEDS OF OUR DREAMS

In the garden, when we water the soil knowing that **weeds** may rise, we can let them come up a little, identify them and see what their intention in the garden is (peaceful coexistence or hostile takeover), then respond accordingly. This sense of awareness and early identification allows us to recognise the weeds that could damage or destroy our seedling and pull them out by the roots.

Similarly, as we take steps toward our dream, we need to keep our eyes open to notice what else emerges as a result of the dream seed being planted, which may ultimately compete with or put the dream at risk. **Weeds** may rise in the form of self-doubt or criticism, they may surface as a friend or colleague that pushes in, judges or overrides the early energy of a dream. It could be a competing priority with your 'day job' or an individual whose personal fears, doubts or jealousy are being exposed and triggered by your commitment to the dream.

We should be watchful, curious and thankful as early weeds rise, for they are showing us what has the potential to hold us back and what could prevent our dreams from growing to their full fruition.

In a healthy, thriving garden, as the roots of our seedlings strengthen and the leaves and flowers grow, conflicting forces such as weeds have less room to emerge and less of an impact when they do. Likewise with our dreams, as our commitment and connection to the vision grows, there is less room for distraction and destructive forces, and we become way more resilient towards any force which may challenge or oppose the dream. But in the early days, we need to be vigilant and we need to be willing to take the time to understand the forces that rise around our dreams so that we can accurately assess which are complementary forces, aligned with our growth in the direction of our dream, and which are

contradictory forces that may need to be chopped out or pulled up
by the roots!

LETTING THEM RISE, LETTING THEM GO

Just as weed seeds may lay dormant from past seasons until conditions
are primed for them to rise, our own doubts and fears are often based
on past experience and may rest quietly within until we begin to step
forward, outside our comfort zone, and trigger them to rise.

As we reach certain thresholds in the dream journey, we may find our
mind and body flooded with anxious thoughts and feelings based on
'what happened last time' or other related memories.

If we know ahead of time that this is likely going to happen, we can keep
an eye out for these fears and feelings, see them not as deterrents but as
motivating forces. When they rise, we can take time to understand them,
to breathe through them, see them for what they are and then gently
disentangle them from our dream. Trying to supress these thoughts or
push them away will often cause them to increase in volume in our mind.
In most cases we are better to draw them out, thank them for the gift
they bring and then let them go (at the roots).

❧

*Growing up as a freestyle skier, aerials was one of my favourite events,
but it was also one of the activities that brought up the greatest amount
of fear. Having had a few big and scary falls growing up, I often found
that in the morning of a big event, before my first jump of the day, my
mind would flood with visions of the worst falls I'd ever had. My whole
body would tense up, become stiff and full of fear. Sometimes I could 'cut
these thoughts off' by focusing harder on the jump I was preparing for.
But often, unless I acknowledged the fear, it would just get stronger and*

louder in my mind until I almost felt paralysed. Not the ideal state to be in when preparing to fly down the inrun and off a giant ramp into the sky.

One day, as I was trying to prepare for a major event and the weeds of fear were strangling my focus, I could feel the pressure rising inside of me until I simply could not contain it anymore. In that instant, I forced a big breath and just gave into it for a moment, proclaiming out loud, "Wow. I feel really scared!" Strangely, as I stopped trying to fight the fear and instead just allowed myself to feel it for a moment, suddenly I felt a massive release of pressure in my whole body. I took another deep breath and said it again, and this time I could feel its stranglehold on my mind begin to release. It was as though by simply acknowledging and giving voice to the fear, it gave it a chance to move out of my body into the air where I could recognise it for what it was — a protective mechanism just trying to keep me safe. I was able to appreciate the fear and thank it for helping me to be extra vigilant and focused in my preparation. Then I was able to turn my attention in the direction of the jump I was preparing for. Thirty seconds later, I successfully completed the jump and strengthened the growth of my dream, having pulled the 'weed of fear' up from the roots.

∛

Giving voice to the fears and doubts as they rise allows us to appreciate the role these forces play, before releasing them and channelling that energy with greater strength in the direction of our dream.

INTENSIVE PLANTING LEAVES LESS ROOM FOR WEEDS

Obstacles are what we see when we take our eyes off the vision.

Last year, we were experimenting with intensive-planting patterns, and we planted a whole bed of lettuce and salad greens super close together (two to three inches apart, instead of the recommended spacing which is three times that). A few weeks of water and sun and the entire raised garden bed literally became a carpet of salad green, with not a single weed or competitive plant in the bed. All available energy in this part of the garden was going directly into the salad seedlings we'd planted and there was simply no space, sunshine or energy for anything else. It was incredible. The only challenge was when these beautiful salad greens ripened, we suddenly had 80+ heads of lettuce, rocket and mustard greens ready to be eaten all at once!

Interestingly, during this same season, my son Josh had entered a very focused dream-growing phase, producing his first album of music. Josh has always been highly immersive by nature — when he finds something he loves, he literally pours all his focus and energy into it. In the case of music, his intensive dream planting equated to 16–18 hours of focused production each day. As the salad bed seedlings dominated every inch of the garden bed, Josh's thoughts and energy dialled in so intensively on the music he was producing that there was zero space for anything else — a little food and a little sleep, but that was about it. For those near Josh, this may have seemed extreme, even selfish at times. But for those who have walked the path of dreams, there was a natural acknowledgement and appreciation that this intensive planting was just what was needed to bring forth his vision in its purest form. Over the course of a full growing season (about six months), Josh completed his first album (which is awesome!) and is now in the process of being launched. Josh is moving into his next season — the sharing of this harvest in the world (more on harvesting later).

Anyone who has galvanised the energy required to create an album, write a book, make a film or develop a major body of work knows that while this level of intensive focus may not be sustainable for all seasons of life, there are times when undiluted immersion is what is required to produce the outcomes we are committed to creating. This was the case with our intensive salad bed (we will do this again!), with Josh's first album, and here—at 1:08 am on a Saturday night—with my own focused commitment to finish this chapter. ☺

SOME WEEDS CHALLENGE, SOME WEEDS HELP

Some are dreams in disguise.

As we take steps on the dream path, there will most certainly be forces that rise to challenge, entangle and potentially draw energy away from our dream. These 'dream weeds' may take root on the inside—in the soil of our being—in the form of fear, resistance, procrastination or distraction. They may also surface on the outside as roadblocks, setbacks, rejection, conflicting opinions, power struggles and jealousy of those in our field. Like some of the running grasses that weave their way across our garden paths, dream weeds may sneak in undetected and run so close to the roots of our dream that we don't notice them until they have our dream surrounded — making it nearly impossible to extract them without the risk of damaging or uprooting the dream itself.

No matter what form dream **weeds** take, the abiding truth—which has revealed itself in the path of dreamers since the beginning of time—is that when we take time (even a few moments) to recognise, authentically address and genuinely release these weeds from our path, we will look back and realise that they ultimately made us stronger. The apparent threat weeds pose to our dream becomes a gift when faced, because it causes us to deepen our resolve, reach a little further, focus more strongly and stand for the lifeforce of our dreams. The dream is what often gets us started on the path, but the **weeds** are there to help us build the resilience and commitment required to fulfil the mission.

Some dream **weeds** test our resolve. Some help us shift our perspective. And some dream weeds ultimately reveal themselves not to be weeds at all, but rather overlooked, underestimated, or misunderstood dreams in their own right.

Sometimes, we set out to reach a specific goal and try very hard to achieve it, and while we may fail to reach the original goal, we discover that from the effort something different or unexpected emerges.
It may first appear that the dream has failed, but what grows instead will ultimately reveal itself as a great expression of the initial intent and often a much more rewarding or fulfilling outcome in the long run.

℘

As a young athlete, all of my dream-building skills and effort were focused on fulfilling a vision of skiing at the Olympics. This was the garden I was growing, and every seed planted, water bucket filled, mulch pile stirred was in service of this dream. When the forces of nature (and the limits of my own body) collided in the form of major injury, this was beyond a weed — it was a bulldozer. But when the whispered call to begin coaching began to surface in my field, the dandelion that rose in the empty soil of the broken dream was deep, strong and healing in a way that I never could have imagined.

Flash forward three decades and I can see now that the seed of my Olympic dream as an athlete was overgrown by injury, but what ultimately emerged were the roots of my path as a coach, which not only delivered the Olympic harvest I was looking for in a different form than

I could have imagined (as the head coach of the Australian Olympic Team), but prepared the soil of my life for an entire career of dream seed cultivation with teams and leaders, artists, athletes and entrepreneurs globally.

SOME THINGS WE PLANT ACT LIKE WEEDS

While there certainly are cases where the aggressive growth of a weed can suppress the growth of an otherwise-healthy garden, there are also cases where a seed we've planted on purpose can completely take over and dominate the garden in ways that aren't healthy.

∾

It's the end of summer as I write this. We have had several weeks of steady rain with very few clear windows to be out tending the garden, so the summer crops have reached their peak and some of them are literally going mad. Tomatoes, pumpkins, zucchini, passionfruit … all foods we love; but they are currently monopolising space across the garden beds, along the fences, into tree branches and across footpaths.

The vines of just three pumpkin plants have now completely taken over the lower quadrant of our garden, leaving no room for anything else to grow. The passionfruit vines have covered the outer fence like a blanket, blocking light from reaching every other plant along the fence. Cherry tomato vines are hugging our chilli bushes like octopus and the zucchinis have eclipsed two of our garden paths, making it impossible for humans to pass. We cherish the fruit that come from each of these plants, but if we are not watchful, they will take over and supress the growth of every other plant in the garden.

So, when we consider the forces that may disrupt the balance and growth cycle of our garden, it's important to consider that sometimes even the very things we are trying to grow can become a threat to the growth and balance of others. And likewise, our passionate pursuit of a dream may so powerfully consume our time, focus and energy that it overrides, undernourishes or threatens the vitality of other key aspects of life. Personal relationships, basic responsibilities and even our own health may swing out of balance under the pursuit of a big dream or vision. For short bursts or peak seasons, this is almost to be expected. When the pumpkin patch flourishes, we make space for it to do so. When an athlete prepares for the Olympics, time with family, friends and outside life changes shape.

But ultimately, we are aiming for seeds to grow in balance with (not in contrast to) the greater garden ecosystem. And likewise, our aim must be for our dreams to rise and flourish in a way that contributes to (not drains) the greater tapestry of our life. As we survey the garden of our dreams, we must be watchful that the dream itself is not acting like a weed — choking out or overriding other key elements or people in our life. The dream may stretch us (and others) well beyond our perceived limits. It may swing us out of balance for periods of time. But in time, the ultimate test of the dream will be its ability to give life and energy to everything and everyone else in the garden.

REFLECTION

- When you think about the life you are living and the seeds you are most committed to growing, what are the strongest **weeds** (inside or out) you currently face, pulling energy away from what you are trying to create?

- What is the biggest potential obstacle to your growth and progress? What if you knew that this obstacle was actually a gift?

- What fear, perception or belief could get in the way of your dream growing to fruition? What would it look like to authentically face this rising force and release it from the roots?

ACTION

1. Spend an hour (or a morning) weeding your actual garden.
   If you don't have a garden, weed a friend's garden. Take time
   to understand the relationship between the plants that were
   intended to grow and those that are strongest in the soil.
   See if you can find at least one 'weed' that is serving an
   unexpected purpose in the life of the garden.

2. Make a list of all the elements (internal and external) that show
   up as **weeds** on your dream-growing journey. What holds you
   back, tangles you up, supresses your lifeforce or takes more than
   it gives? Examine these weeds with discernment and take time
   to consider, "What gifts do these weeds bring to me and my
   dream journey? How will they make me stronger and clearer
   in my resolve?"

3. What actions could you take in the next 24 hours to help
   you get to the root cause and release whatever is challenging
   your dream?

8.

ADAPT
(+ RECEIVE HELP FROM UNEXPECTED SOURCES)

When patterns are broken, new worlds emerge.

TULI KUPFERBERG

Last year, we decided we wanted to grow blueberries. We'd never grown blueberries, so we devoted an entire section in our new garden to the little guys. Our region is not the best for blueberries, but we were pretty determined. So, we loaded up the soil with everything we thought would help, along with heaps of our own compost, worm tea, coffee grounds (yes, they help too), etc.

In the end, the blueberries did okay. Ash, Josh and the birds pretty much picked and ate each individual blueberry as it arrived, but we had some progress. And I do think they will do better next season. However, in the meantime something quite extraordinary happened all around them ...

As mentioned, we mixed our compost into the garden bed to give the blueberries and extra boost. That compost—which originally started out as fruit and vegetable scraps from our kitchen—must've had a few pumpkin seeds in it (perhaps more than a few). While we were keeping an eye out for the arrival of each new blueberry, the pumpkins (about 30 of them) began quietly, voluntarily rising up and weaving their vines across the garden. We didn't consciously plan for or plant the pumpkins, but while we were busy striving to grow the thing we thought we wanted, something else grew in its place without any help from us — delivering a thriving bounty of the perfect winter vegetable, just in time for winter, when we would really need it!

We're currently having some form of pumpkin with almost every meal (roasted, baked, steamed, bread, muffins, pies and soup). If you happen to visit our house for any reason at all, you will most likely leave with a pumpkin.

And so, we find that this journey of growing gardens and dreams has many unexpected twists and turns, often requiring us to make dynamic adjustments in our expectations and our actions and along the way. Sometimes, in the process of cultivating the seeds of one thing, we

*unknowingly plant the seeds of something else alongside it. And while
it may take absolutely all our effort and skill to nurture and coax the
growth of one project or idea, others (like the pumpkin) seem to rise up
into our lap, bringing gifts to our garden (often way more than we could
imagine) without much effort on our part, except to harvest.*

*As an athlete pursuing my Olympic dream, I threw everything I had
into the training, prep and focus on my path. Each breakthrough result
or podium finish was like coaxing an individual blueberry from the
soil. Each was hard-won and appreciated, but the path was lonely and
in constant need of composting, churning and boosting. What I didn't
realise at the time, was that while I was pushing and striving for my
own individual results, I was also building a foundation for what was
waiting to grow naturally and abundantly inside of me — my path as a
coach (the pumpkin). As a sort of team captain, I was often in 'coaching
conversations' with fellow athletes, simply because I cared, and we were
on the same journey together. Over time, these conversations deepened
naturally until the bulldozer of injury ultimately revealed to me that
while I had put my conscious effort into growing the elite athlete in me,
the long-term soil of my garden bed was much more conducive to growing
the coach.*

☙

Sometimes, when we are fixated on one outcome or goal, it can be easy
to miss the alternative path that life is offering us — even if it is more of
a match for who we are (and what we really want deep down). It took me
two blown-out knees and multiple surgeries to recognise that the soil of
my dream as an athlete was, in the long run, more naturally rich with the
nutrients of a coach. We could have dug up the pumpkins when they first
started growing to save the blueberry patch, but as a result of trusting
nature, we actually ended up with a healthy harvest of both!

"FULL SUN" DOESN'T MEAN IT WON'T BURN

Recently, I was visiting my family in the US during a very hot summer in the northern hemisphere. Both of my brothers have picked up gardening in the last few years and had some great success with their early efforts, so both committed to expanding their garden beds this year. When I visited, they were excited to share, but were also lamenting that even though they had followed all the same steps this year as they had the previous summer (prep, planting and watering with same amounts and frequency), for some reason almost nothing in the garden was growing as fast or abundantly as the year before.

We took a walk through the beds and the first thing I noticed (which was normal, coming from the subtropics to the mountains) was that the plants and soil looked very thirsty. My brothers commented on how hot and dry the summer had been, but they both had their drip water lines set up just like they had the year before so they couldn't understand why things weren't growing. What we realised—which sounds obvious but can be very easy to overlook —is that every year and season is different! Every crop cycle is unique, and each requires enough personal attention and focus to be able to adapt and make adjustments along the way.

༄

Just because the compass points north doesn't mean the path won't wind up and down along the way. Just because the packet says to plant in full sun, doesn't mean the plant won't dry out or burn when it's hot. The seed packet, good planning and our past experience can all be super helpful in getting us started on the journey, but our ability to stay connected to the pulse of things as they grow, and to **adapt** along the way (even if that means doing things differently than we have in the past) is the difference between a well-planned garden (or dream) and one that thrives and continues to evolve each step of the way.

As a coach of leaders in a variety of industries globally, one of the biggest challenges that I often observe, is how easy it can be to stifle the progress of a team or vision simply because we are trying to do things as we have always done them. It's taken us a lot of effort to get to where we are, so it's natural to want to simply consolidate that learning and apply it to the path forward. As we are looking at areas of the project or organisation that may need to change, our default thinking almost always wants to compare to 'how we did it last time'. This can be a great starting place, but if we are truly committed to doing something more, something different and more expansive than what we have done previously, this automatically puts us into the category of needing to be open to discovering new ways of doing things. This sounds obvious, but the challenge here is that we are often way more comfortable with doing things how we have done them previously, simply because it is what we know.

In order to create something new, something fresh and alive, beyond what we (or others) have done previously, we need to be willing to move beyond the known into new and potentially uncomfortable territory.

On the dream path, it's a great thing to say, "We need to get comfortable with being uncomfortable." But the truth is, this doesn't stop it from feeling uncomfortable.

EMBRACING THE DISCOMFORT OF NOT KNOWING

The opportunity for us as leaders, gardeners and growers of dreams is to start recognising the discomfort of new territory not as an alarm bell that something is wrong (which our sub-conscious may like to indicate) but as a window into an authentic path forward into the realms of the dream. If we can predict everything that happens next, if we know all the answers, this may feel comfortable, but this is not the path to creating something new.

When we don't know the answer and we are willing to rest for a moment, or a season, in that 'not knowing', we get the gift of opening our eyes and senses to a new frontier, beyond our plan and preconceived notions, into what is actually happening and what is actually being called for.

With trust and curiosity, our response in this moment takes us off the well-trodden path of our history and puts us onto the more dynamic ground of what this living dream is telling us now. Our presence, awareness and willingness to respond to this moment with fresh eyes becomes an incredible point of power, enabling us to move forward, often in ways we never would have imagined.

For the leaders of a rapidly growing organisation, sensing an underlying tension in their team can become a catalyst to leave the comfort of their office and spending more time in the field — listening, engaging and discovering new ways forward. For a music producer like my son Josh, the positive edge of his comfort zone (and where he gets the greatest feedback from life) is found in moving from the safe privacy of his studio into playing live to an audience.

For my brothers, the momentary discomfort of realising that last year's drip lines were clogged, and therefore not giving this year's garden what it needed, was quickly remedied by a deep soak and a commitment to do so more often in these hot summer days. No major epiphany required, but a willingness to observe, change and ***adapt***. A simple step for the humans, life changing for the garden.

To keep our dreams alive, moving and growing, we need to be willing to change and ***adapt*** our approach to meet the seasons — not as we expected them to be, but as they are. Just because the packets says, "full sun", doesn't mean the dream won't dry out if we aren't responding to what it's telling us it needs.

Embrace uncertainty.
Some of the most beautiful
chapters in our lives won't
have a title until much later.

BOB GOFF

Questions to Consider About Stepping Beyond Your Comfort Zone

- Consider a dream or present focus in your life. How much is your current approach based on what you know from the past vs genuinely stepping into new personal territory?

- Are there aspects of your past approach that you are comfortable with, but may not be what's needed to get you where you are now committed to going?

- What would it look like for you step beyond what's known or comfortable in order to give your dream the energy it needs to fully thrive?

ACCEPTING HELP FROM UNEXPECTED FORCES

In summertime here, it gets so hot that it can be difficult to grow lettuce without it wilting, burning in the sun or bolting straight to seed (more on seeds later). But we love our salad greens, so every year we do our best to keep them watered and coax them along. This year, unbeknownst to us, our compost soil had some papaya seeds in it and as spring was leaning towards summer, a handful of papaya trees began springing up spontaneously in the garden beds we had set aside for lettuce (a bit like pumpkins growing in the blueberry patch … this may be a trend!).

Because I hadn't planned for papayas to grow right in the middle of the veggie garden, my first inclination was to try to transplant them to another spot. But I decided to stay curious for a moment and see if nature had a reason for them to grow there. We've had difficulty growing papayas in other areas of our land, but they seemed super happy. And I was pretty sure my salad greens were going to struggle in this bed anyway, so I decided to let the papayas stay, and see what would happen.

Within weeks, something amazing did happen. As the summer air started heating up, the young papaya trees shot up to be six to eight feet tall and spread their leaves out like a fan, creating diffused light and shade across the beds. As the flowers bloomed and fruit started to ripen in the full sun of their canopy (which papayas love), the dapple-lit conditions they created in the beds below fostered the perfect environment for the salad greens I had planted to rise up without being blasted by the heat. By mid-summer, the greens were pumping, the papayas were fruiting and everyone in the summer garden was getting what they needed to thrive. Amazing!

The path to fulfilling a dream is a super dynamic journey, with unexpected challenges and also gifts and help from unexpected sources. Gifts we would never have the chance to receive and sources of support we would never know were there until we are on the journey, in the garden, growing with our dream. Things rarely develop exactly as we think they will. But as we combine our commitment to fulfil our mission with a willingness to listen, observe and ***adapt*** to what emerges, and as we open ourselves to receive guidance and support when it arrives (even when we don't expect it), we often find the path unfolds to inspired outcomes in ways that are actually better than what we could have planned for or imagined.

When we start the journey, we hold the seed of our dream in our hand and the vision for its ultimate fruition in our mind. As we step foot on the dream cultivation path, we enter the rhythmic laws of nature, and these are often different than the rules we've been 'trained' to live by in modern life.

If we work with natural law and follow the heartbeat of the dream (as opposed to trying to force the dream to grow 'our way'), what emerges may be different than what we planned, but in the big-picture view of things, it is often more expansive, more inclusive and truer to who we really are.

The plan is enough to get us onto the playing field of our dream, but once we and the dream are moving, we must add dynamic *adaptability* to the commitment and focus we bring. We must find a way to keep our eyes and heart connected to the ultimate vision *and* our fingers on the pulse of how things actually are, how what is actually growing and what is needed next, now, today for our dream to survive and thrive in the world.

We can't get stuck staring at the dream as it wilts in the sun or gets rootbound in a pot, even if the instructions said it would be okay. We have to be willing to get out of our chair, to turn the hose on, to respond, to **adapt**. We have to be willing to let go of how we thought it was going to go, and get fully in tune with how it is going.

If things don't happen easily or if the path we are walking gets uncomfortable, it doesn't mean something's wrong. It may just mean that the dream is growing and it needs us to expand who we are along with it.

The reason we call it a dream is because it takes us to a different realm. A realm beyond what we consider to be our normal day-to-day. The outcome of the dream itself may have great value, but the prevailing gift of any great dream is how it causes *us* to grow on the inside. To expand and remember who we are and what we are capable of.

In the garden, this might mean shifting something out of the sun or into the sun. It might mean building a trellis to support the growth of the dragon fruit, cherry tomatoes or beans. Or in the case of our salad greens and papayas, it might mean planting one thing, but watching another grow much stronger in its place before revealing its purpose in the greater whole.

In the nurturing of a dream, this may mean shifting our pace, intensity and focus. This may mean waking up earlier, reaching out to new people, putting immense energy into one path or product only to discover a completely unexpected opportunity rises in its place.

There are times when what is needed is for us to stick with the plan, be consistent, disciplined and stay the course, no matter what. There are also times when what is needed is for us to radically **adapt**, evolve or depart from our known way of doing things.

There are times when the growing of a dream requires quiet, private focus, and there are times when the only way forward is to open up to the insight and contribution of others. It is easy to think that if the dream seed started in our hands, we are the only ones who can take it forward. But, as the dream garden grows, we may find the opposite to be true. By trying to do it all on our own, by sticking with how we've always done things, we run the risk of starving or stifling the very thing we wish to grow.

LEARNING TO RECEIVE

Accepting help is a gift to the giver.

ANONYMOUS

Many of us are reluctant to ask for or receive help. I don't know why exactly, but our conditioning tells us that we're the one who needs to do all the heavy lifting. We may think that reaching out for help shows weakness, or perhaps we are afraid of burdening others with more to do. Strangely, in many cases, the absolute opposite is true. When we call upon, empower and engage others to contribute their unique part to a dream, we not only unleash the greater potential of the dream itself (to grow beyond us as individuals), but we give people an opportunity to awaken their own sense of purpose, of being valued for who they are and the dream seeds that may be germinating inside them.

I could have tried to build our market garden by myself and maybe eventually I would have achieved a result. But by inviting a band of young humans to help, not only did we set the garden up *way* faster and better than I ever could have done alone, everyone learned a ton and continues to feel proudly part of the dream. Plus, they all have a lifetime 'membership' to harvest food whenever they visit, which they do often!

If the dream you are growing is alive, by the very laws of nature there will always be a need to ***adapt*** to the moment, to respond to change, to embrace challenge and accept help from both seen and unseen forces. You may not ever get comfortable outside of your comfort zone, but you can build confidence and skills out there in the new frontier and learn to recognise the unknown and unexpected as carriers of great gifts.

Trust is key here. Active, dynamic, responsive trust. Trust that simultaneously believes in the deeper calling of the dream AND remains open to shifting gears, changing approach and discovering what's at the heart of this calling that we may not have realised or imagined possible when we started.

REFLECTION

- How do you respond when things don't go according to your 'plan'? Do you dig in harder, even if it means forcing the way? Or are you open to seeing what else life may have in store?

- Have you had the experience of pushing hard for one outcome or result, only to discover a different, more fitting (more abundant) path emerging?

- What is currently growing in your life that you didn't consciously plant, but could be a great ally, gift or doorway if your eyes were open to seeing it that way?

- What would it look like for you to reach out, include or 'accept help' from someone else in the service of your dream?

ACTION

1. Spend time curiously observing your garden, what you have intended to grow and how it is evolving with the seasons and ecosystem around it. Where do you need to **adapt** your approach to enable a fresh wave of growth?

2. Consider your current approach to your dream and how it is growing and evolving from when you first started it.

   - Identify one aspect of your approach that you need to **adapt** or change in order to allow fresh opportunity or breakthrough. Make this shift this week!

   - Identify at least one person you could reach out to in service of your dream. Make contact, call a meeting, call on their greatness and ask for help!

9.

HARVEST
(+ SHARE, PRESERVE & ALCHEMISE)

What you get by
achieving your goal
is not as important as
who you become by
achieving your goal.

ZIG ZIGLAR

I've always loved chilli. That warm combo of slap-in-the-face and hug that comes with a well-spiced taco, pasta sauce or stir fry is often what brings a dish to life for me — even if it hurts a little or makes me sweat. My son Josh has grown up with a steady stream of chillies in his diet and has developed an appetite for spice way beyond my own. As a result, when we first laid out our market garden, an array of chilli bush seedlings were some of the first to be planted in a row, right down the centre of one of the beds. Eight to ten bushes ranging from tasty Thai red chilli and cayenne peppers, to the zesty punch of birdseye and habanero, right through to the genuinely dangerous, high voltage Trinidad Scorpion and Carolina Reaper (#1 and #2 hottest in the world).

The garden was new, and we were excited. At the time, 'the more the better' seemed like the right approach. We'd had success with chilli bushes previously so we were confident they would grow well. But we didn't plan for each seedling to burst forth with 50–100 chillies in their first season. That's over 500 chillies for a three-person family … and they just keep growing. Yikes!

Simultaneously, we'd been going for it with flowering herbs (basil, rosemary, thyme, etc.), medicinal flowering trees (lemon myrtle, aniseed myrtle, acacia), citrus up in the apiary for the bees, and a couple of our native Davidson plum trees were really starting to pump, with hundreds of little plums going ripe along the trunk.

As the seasons would have it, many of these seedlings, bushes and trees came to full fruition around the same time and suddenly we went from being really excited by how quickly everything was growing, to genuinely overwhelmed by the complex challenge of what to do with it all now that it was ready for harvest!

At first, we just walked around and stared at this bounty with a combination of deep appreciation and slight panic. We'd spent so much

*time planning, preparing, dreaming, digging, planting, watering
and weeding, we never really thought about what to do once it was
all producing.*

*But when the first of the habaneros (our favourite of the chillies) started
to show signs of over-ripening and falling from the tree, a sense of real
responsibility kicked in and we knew we had to respond. We had to shift
from the focus and commitment needed to cultivate and grow the garden,
into the harvesting, enjoying, preserving and sharing of the fruit.*

*The next few weeks involved a hilarious combination of collecting,
sampling, blending, drying, infusing and concocting chillies, herbs and
fruit — resulting in a bizarre variety of sauces, jams and chutneys,
infused oils, smoking-hot tequilas and citrus plum wines. Tearfully spicy
tasting sessions with Josh's friends, jarred gifts for house visitors (whether
they wanted them or not) and entrepreneurial visions for 101 ways to
use dried organic chilli flakes were all part of our first real chilli season,
waking us up to the power of the **harvest**.*

[This is] a time to harvest
human potential.

SADHGURU

HARVESTING YOUR DREAM: A VITALLY IMPORTANT STEP

There are many seasons in the dream-growing journey and for the most part if we are paying attention, each step often leads naturally, one way or another, to the next. There are moments when a dream is just an idea. There are moments when the dream is just beginning, when we are working so hard, but it feels out of reach … and there are moments when the dream is mature enough that it calls for *harvest*, release, celebration and enjoying the fruits.

Some would say that harvesting the fruit of our completed dream is the ultimate aim. Yet, amidst our modern, busy world and the mission of doing everything we need to do to keep moving on the path, the moment of *harvest* is also easy to overlook, take for granted or completely miss. We are so busy thinking about what needs to be planted next that we miss the moment when our dream has come to fruition and is offering us the magic of its fruit.

It is often said that the journey, not the destination, matters most in our endeavours. In this way, we can truly say that one of the great reasons for fulfilling the dream is because of the growth, discovery and experience we gain along the way. Nonetheless, the *harvest* remains an essential step on this path. It is an opportunity to acknowledge, appreciate and get caught up with what we have created and with who we have become during the journey.

We don't climb the mountain only to reach the peak. We climb first to have the experience of being on the mountain. Reaching the summit may be the ultimate goal when we start, but looking back we will see that the main reason for summiting was in order to have the fullest experience of being on the mountain.

We don't grow the tree (or dream) only for the **harvest**, but we can (and must) **harvest** to complete the circle, honour our partnership and appreciate the journey we have been on together.

DREAMS RIPEN IN DIFFERENT WAYS, AT DIFFERENT TIMES

Outside our kitchen we have a little herb garden with a sampling of most of the herbs we use in our cooking, teas and other alchemical potions. Herbs are unique because they produce quickly and perpetually throughout the course of their sometimes-multi-year long lives. Interestingly with herbs, it's the regular pruning, harvesting and sharing that actually help to stimulate continued healthy, bushy growth.

Moving up into the main garden we have a range of greens and vegetables that normally grow to fruition over the course of a single season. Some, like broccoli or cauliflower, put all their energy into growing a single head of fruit, while others like beans, zucchini, cucumber, tomatoes will produce a whole wave of fruit over the season. The lettuces we graze upon leaf by leaf, giving them a chance to regenerate and continue growing along the way. The celery we harvest twice over two seasons.

∽

Like herbs and leafy greens, some dreams benefit from intense focus, iteration and rapid harvest in order to produce consistent results in the short term (think of a writer who produces and delivers several articles or posts each week). Other seeds in our dream garden may have equal or greater capacity to grow and yield fruit, but require more consistent effort over an extended period of time (that same writer focuses on one key topic to complete a book in three to six months).

Some of us are natural sprinters, some middle-distance runners and some are built for endurance. Likewise, certain dreams have different lengths and phases which may call for different aspects of ourselves to bring them to completion and deliver. It can be helpful to notice and distinguish what type of dream you are working on and the specific energy (intensity, pace and length of time) that may be required to bring it to fruition.

໑

Moving out from the veggie garden into the citrus orchard, the stone fruit and bananas, these fruit trees all start producing annual harvests within the first two years of life, growing fuller and more abundant with season — especially if they are well nourished, pruned and maintained along the way.

And as we reach the outer edges of our upper field, we find the avocados, macadamias and pecans. These trees were planted when they were young and they have been growing slow and steady, sending their roots down and out as far as possible before they rise into the giants they will one day become. They may not start fruiting until four to six years after planting, but once they begin, they will provide annual harvests that could fill a truck, while offering branches to climb, hang swings from and picnic beneath for generations to come.

And so it is that within a hundred metres of our back door we have a full and dynamic variety of trees and plants growing, each of which has its own life cycle and fruiting season. Some rise to fruition within a few weeks and dissolve back into the soil before the next season, while others take time to grow and mature before giving their fruit for decades to come. All are needed and each adds a unique element to the garden of our life.

In life, we may be working on several different projects, aspirations or visions at one time. Some, like the salad greens, are momentary, short-term endeavours, but they feed us and help keep our energy building. Whenever I write and share an article, produce and release a short video, facilitate a workshop, coaching session or leadership meeting, I feel like I am 'in the salad garden' of my work. Each of these forms of expression are only one small piece in themselves, but together they form a creative network that builds and shares energy while feeding my family (literally and figuratively).

When I spend time on strategic partnerships and longer-term engagements with teams and organisations, I find myself moving into the citrus orchard and banana grove of my dream landscape. More thought and upfront planning are required. More patience and steady cultivation are called for, but as these visions move into fruition the scale and longevity of the work and the breadth of its outcome start to expand and multiply. A video series grows into a multi-layered program which can be launched, shared and repeated each year. A workshop or leadership-team launch grows into a multi-year, full-team/project engagement focused on reaching and empowering every person across an organisation.

And, as I sit here typing these words of a book that has been growing roots inside of me for many years, it is as though I am adding mulch and trimming the branches of one of the avocado trees we've nurtured from seed over an extended period in our upper field. It's taken longer than we may have imagined for this tree to grow to maturity, but when it is ready to be harvested and shared, its fruit—and the seeds held within—have capacity to well outlive the author and continue growing in the lives and dream gardens of all who connect with it.

HARVESTING GIFTS ALONG THE PATH

In a rich, dream-filled life, we may have many layers and forms of dreams growing at any given time and the role of the *harvest* is woven through all of them. Not to celebrate a win too early or pull us out of the flow, but to bring more enjoyment and momentum to the journey and help us continue to grow. As we validate the steps we have taken, as we pause to experience the fruit of our efforts, the path itself becomes sweeter and our steps upon it become stronger and more confident. If we never pause to appreciate the steps we are taking, if we choose never to *harvest* until the very end, we may miss many ripe experiences and milestones and the fruits of our dream may fall to waste.

A musician's dream spans from the simple melody he hums on his morning walk, to the opus he will one day write to inspire audiences around the world. An artist captures a spontaneous sketch in their journal every day on the train, while simultaneously spending years on a major body of work in their studio. An ecology student matches research discoveries in the lab with long afternoons walking amongst trees. A young entrepreneur harvests the difficult lessons learned in her first job, while developing the business plan for a global social enterprise and her life path as a leader.

Here on our land, now that we have spent the time and energy to plant the many hundreds of seeds and seedlings we are growing, one of my favourite activities is to simply stroll around the field and through the garden, tending to what needs attention and grazing on whatever I notice is ripe and ready to be eaten. I call it 'The Salad Walk' and sometimes I do this two to three times daily. This is not a distraction from the 'real work' of growing the dream. This helps me stay connected and responsive to the pulse of the land, while being fed along the way.

In this way, I not only receive the most alive nutrients imaginable (literally straight from the ground into my body), I also learn where my energy is needed, I discover which plants, trees and fruits are ready to *harvest* and which need extra support.

Translate this into the sporting arena and we see a coach who is so connected to her team that she misses no opportunity to validate and call out the daily effort and breakthroughs each player has in preparation for a big event. In the business world we see managers who spend enough time connecting with and appreciating the progress and milestones of their team that a quiet momentum builds, where each person feels valued for their unique part in a shared vision. A drummer smiles and nods at the free expression of guitar player's solo. A parent pauses their multi-tasking meal preparation to listen to their child share a story. These are all forms of *harvest*. Some are momentary but the ripple effects of pausing to appreciate and 'glean the fruit' of a moment can stay with us for a lifetime.

When we give ourselves permission to live in the arena of our dreams, the question is usually not, "When will our *harvest* come?" But rather, "What is here in our field of dreams, ready to be harvested now?"

If we can recognise and appreciate the simple steps, the little wins as they rise to fruition, we will feel a sense of momentum building towards the bigger picture while enjoying and celebrating each turn in the path along the way.

Questions to Consider About Gifts Along the Path

- Scanning the different aspects of your life, work and dream-building endeavour, what do you notice about the progress, growth and potential to **harvest now**?

- What would it look to take 'The Salad Walk' and appreciate the aspects of your dream that are growing well, already achieved, ready to be collected and enjoyed?

DON'T PICK TOO SOON, DON'T PICK TOO LATE

We had some friends over last week, building beehives and working in the garden. Late afternoon, we were walking through the field admiring everything that was growing and one person in the group noticed a huge papaya that was just turning ripe, almost perfect for picking. I was about to tell him to go ahead and pick it (knowing that it would finish ripening off the tree), but I got distracted and forgot to mention it. The next morning when I went out to water the garden, that almost-perfect papaya had been almost completely eaten by critters in the night!

In this subtropical region, when it comes to several of the most magical fruit varieties (mango, papaya, guava, banana) there is a super-fine line between being almost perfect and being eaten by a bird, bat or possum in the night. As these fruit varieties come into season, it becomes a day-by-day, hour-by-hour mission to monitor their growth to make sure they reach full maturity, without over-ripening or attracting a thieving community member in the night. Pick them too soon and you miss their true sweetness, wait too long and you may miss them altogether.

☙

The same can be true of our most special projects and dreams. Sometimes the expectations of others, our desire for approval or our anxiousness to move on to what's next can leave us feeling pressured to release or share a dream before it is ready. On the other hand, and particularly with artistic endeavours, it can be easy to push our dreams past their prime. To keep working them (or over-work them) even when they are ready, with a desire to make them more perfect.

Our job as the dream grower is to recognise the timing of the dream as it comes into ripeness and to seize the moment when the energy of the dream is at its peak. Sometimes it is clear and obvious, but if the journey has been long and challenging, it can be difficult to let go or even to know when it is time to complete. Having worked in the film industry for several years, I've often heard it said that the filmmaking process is never finished, it simply ends when the filmmakers run out of time or money.

Some of us become so accustomed to the effort, drive and focus required to grow the dream that we resist pausing long enough to **_harvest_** the gifts or recognise when a phase or milestone is complete. We can get stuck in a pattern of finishing one thing and moving quickly on to the next, so as not to lose momentum or risk dropping the ball. But the greater risk is that we miss the opportunity to appreciate and learn from the steps we have taken, we miss the chance to acknowledge those who have helped along the way, and we miss the power that comes when we allow ourselves—for a moment—to breathe deep and feel the energy of being 'complete'.

WHO ARE WE TO JUDGE?

As a writer, I've had interesting experiences when I've almost finished with a piece of writing but have run out of time to do a final polish and have to hand it over. Strangely, I often later discover that the bits and pieces I would have edited out if I had had the time to make one final pass are some of the elements that readers acknowledge and appreciate the most.

In my last screenwriting project, the director and I recognised this tendency and actually set up our creative process to allow for it. Whenever I was doing a final polish on a scene, I would mark the lines that I wanted to change but leave the original in the script for others to read. Often, what resonated most for the reader was a mix of my final tweaks and the unedited version.

&

Even if we believe our dreams still need more ripening, sometimes that last 5 per cent of a dream is best ripened 'off the vine', in the sharing with others we trust. And while we may want our dream to be impeccable, sometimes it's the imperfections that make the dream accessible and alive to those who will encounter it next. And most importantly, it keeps the dream moving. If we tinker and fine tune too much, we run the risk of trimming out the humanness, the pulse.

Part of this final step, part of the **harvest** is knowing what is our job and what can others do better, faster, even truer than us?

Recently I sat with a friend who is finishing an album. The tracks had all been mixed and mastered and the only thing left was to choose how they would be ordered on the album. He knew that himself and the sound engineer were the only ones who would know when the tracks themselves were ready. But once each song was complete, he realised that the ordering of the tracks would influence the experience of listening to the album. So, his way of ripening his final decision was to listen to the album with a handful of trusted friends and gain their view of the experience. This was his way of loosening his hold on the ripening fruit and allowing others to help separate it from the vine.

Questions to Consider About Letting Yourself Harvest

- What visions or ideas have been on the vine long enough, perhaps at risk of over-ripening because of your perfectionism or reluctance to release them to the world?

- Where is the ripest dream in your life right now? What would it look like for you to let go of your 'hold' on the process and allow this **harvest** into your life?

THE FRUIT THAT FALLS AT YOUR FEET

At the base of a few of the avocado trees (mentioned above) we've planted passionfruit vines because while we wait years for the avos to come through, we can enjoy passionfruit abundantly in one season. They are hearty, beautiful to look at and they like to climb, making the avocado, with its strong, climbable branches, a perfect partner. One of the things I love the most about passionfruit (besides the fact that they taste amazing) is that when they are ripe, they are super easy to pick and, in most cases, they literally fall to ground, (undamaged due to their thick outer skin), ready to be collected, sliced open and devoured.

❧

In life, amidst our efforts to build energy towards our longer-term dreams, it can be easy to overlook ripening opportunities that may be growing right in front of us. In our efforts to achieve something great on the outside, we often overlook the qualities we already have on the inside ready to **_harvest_** and deploy. As a coach and mentor, something I find most fascinating while working with leaders and humans of many different walks, is how often people overlook their natural greatness — aspects of themselves that are right in front of or within them, so obvious and clear that they don't even recognise them as strengths or gifts.

We are so conditioned to believe that what is needed to achieve our dreams is something outside of ourselves. We think that in order to get what we really want, we need to be, do or have something more, better or different than who we naturally are. I'll say that again:

We think that in order to get what we really want, we need to be, do or have something more, better or different than who we naturally are.

It's a mouthful but it's also a major barrier to harvesting our dreams.

Because of this, our own low-hanging fruit—the qualities, strengths, perspectives and experiences we have naturally right here within us— are often ignored, overlooked or undervalued. In our efforts to achieve greatness we tend to massively underestimate our greatest asset — who we are. Just as we are. Exactly who we are. Right here and now.

The seasons of your life have brought you to this moment and if you are standing (or sitting, lying or floating) here, by the very nature of making it this far, there are aspects of you that are ripe, full and ready for the **_harvest_**. It is easy to think that once we achieve the thing, then we can own and appreciate the qualities that got us there. In most cases, the opposite is true. Once we clearly claim and appreciate who we are, we unlock our natural ability to achieve the thing.

Questions to Consider About Your Innate Greatness

- What is one quality you possess that others appreciate and admire, but you see as "nothing special" because it's just the way you are?

- If you were to harness and fully harvest this quality as one of your dream-building superpowers, how might it help empower your path?

SHARING THE HARVEST (AKA THE ART OF 'SHIPPING')

Some of us are great creators but not natural promoters, marketers or business operators. We pour our energy into the planting and growing of the dream, but when it comes time to **harvest** and share it with the world, we either constrict the flow with perfectionism—telling ourselves and others the dream is not ready—or we simply fail to pour the same level of passion and energy into the sharing of the dream as we did in the creation of it.

We end up with a finished, ripened dream, undelivered. Like a guava tree laden with unpicked fruit, we become heavy, bowed down and stuck. We start to question the value of the dream and/or our ability to deliver it. Our fear of appearing 'salesy' or cheapening the integrity of the dream by stepping out and promoting it, results in a kind of humble reluctance that does not honour the original seed or the journey that we have been on together. Unless something or someone shakes us free of this paranoia, we will soon find the fruits of our labour withering on the vine, and with it our confidence and commitment to share our dream outward with the world.

There is one simple antidote to this risk of over-cooking, over-ripening and stagnating the ***harvest*** of our dream. In the words of my friend and author Seth Godin, we simply have to "ship it". We have to galvanise the energy of the dream when it is alive and kicking and we have to send it out into the world. We have to get good at shipping.

In this moment of ***harvest***—when we are being called to shift from artist and dream grower to entrepreneur, performer or business owner … from canvases and paints to event planning, posters and travel logistics … from creating to delivering—there are a few keys that may help navigate these vitally important steps. There are some principles that can help us 'ship'. They are similar to what was recently required to help us ***harvest*** a truckload of chillies:

1. Reconnect with why you planted this dream in the first place, and why this dream chose you to be its grower.

2. Remember that this dream grew for you and with you, so harvesting its gifts is part of completing the partnership you have with your dream.

3. Ask for help! As we said before, "Accepting help is a gift to the giver," and there may be others in your world whose skills and passions are perfect for what you need to help put this dream out into the world.

4. Ship it! When you have taken the time and energy to grow a dream to fruition, it becomes a responsibility to ***harvest*** and share the fruit. You can be discerning about who you share with (at least at first), but it must be shared!

What happens when a goal is scored on the soccer field? What happens when a musician finishes a song on stage? What happens in the space between verses of a poem or the gap between courses in a beautiful meal?

These are moments of meaningful pause when we **harvest** the gifts of our dream. Taking time to honour, enjoy and share the fruit is an essential part of the dream-growing journey.

You may be working hard to bring one dream to fruition while others ripen on their own. Whether or not the path has unfolded just as you planned, doesn't make it any less miraculous. Notice what is growing, notice what is coming to fruition and don't miss the opportunity to **harvest**, appreciate and share.

REFLECTION

Getting Caught Up with Who You've Become

- Make a list of things (dreams, people, projects) that are currently alive in your life or work that didn't exist for you five years ago, but started as an idea, inkling, impulse or vision.

- Consider which of these seedlings were carefully planned and cultivated from seed, which ones arrived into your care already in motion and which ones you didn't even realise were growing until they began bearing fruit.

- Keep going on the list to include new, special people in your life, hobbies you have picked up, new skills or qualities you've developed. Consider goals you've set yourself and important tasks you've completed. When have you hatched a plan, heard a spontaneous call or embraced an invitation and you have followed it to fruition? These are all part of your dream garden. Take a moment to recognise and appreciate as many of these as you can think of — and then think some more.

- What about times that you may have participated in the cultivating of someone else's dream? When have you helped a friend go past their comfort zone (and joined them) in service to a special project. Think of when you've done something for someone without asking, maybe without them even knowing, but you did it because you saw a fresh seed sprouting and you knew it needed watering. This someone could be a friend, a stranger, a team member, an animal or the environment you live in. Each of these beings have evolutionary impulses and dreams of their own. When we bring ourselves into their field with intent to serve, we naturally become woven into the seedling dreams that are ready to come through them.

Consider how you have contributed to others' dreams, big and small, and take a moment to appreciate yourself, and life, for that.

ACTION

1. Following the above reflection, make a list of people who have made a real positive difference to your dream or life journey (please make sure YOU are also on this list).

2. In the next 24 hours, reach out to these people and acknowledge them for the specific contribution they have made and the impact they have had on your life or your dream.

3. *Harvest* whatever is ripe and ready in your actual garden (flowers, herbs, vegetables, fruit), and give these living beings an opportunity to share their gifts with you. Take the time to enjoy them, share them and celebrate their great expressions in the garden of life.

10.

REST
(FLOWERS, SEEDS …
BEGIN AGAIN)

The chance to be part of
this happens briefly.

The invitation is not
to show how inventive
and imaginative you
are, but how much you
can notice what you are
already a part of.

GUY BURGS

When seeds have been planted, watered and weeded … When seedling plants have risen from the garden bed into ripeness … When fruits and greens have been harvested, enjoyed, shared and digested … We arrive to the end of a season and the beginning of a completion cycle for the seed.

When dream seeds have been transported from the veranda of possibility in our mind, into the soil of action and fruition in our lives … When we have walked the journey of taking an idea from inception and cultivation into delivery, sharing, shipping, releasing and launching it into the world … When we have reaped the harvest of our deep devotion and commitment to our mission, there comes a moment when the next action does not require more doing, but rather taking time to *be*. Taking time to absorb, digest, integrate and get to know the person we have become in the process of growing a dream to fruition.

LET THEM FLOWER

In the gardening world the term 'bolt' is used to describe the moment when a vegetable, herb or green has reached the end of its fruit or leaf-producing cycle and decides it is time to move on. This moment of 'bolting' is often brought on by a dramatic shift in temperature or humidity and signals the change of one season to the next. For the gardener, this means the end of a lettuce or parsley crop. For the plant this signifies an important shift from 'producing' for the season to securing future generations.

❧

I was walking through our herb garden this morning and noticed the coriander/cilantro bush was shooting up and beginning to flower. In our area, coriander grows best in winter and tends to bolt as soon as the days begin to get warmer. It's a bummer to see the end of the coriander for the season, but what happens next is quite miraculous.

Miracle #1 is that as soon as the coriander opens her very first flower and the scent of that flower permeates out into the garden, she begins to attract bees, butterflies and other pollinators to come collect nectar and pollen for the nourishment of their communities. This stimulates the reproductive chemistry of the coriander, causing Miracle #2: thousands of tiny seeds for future coriander bushes to grow.

So, while the season of coriander in our tacos may be complete, the next step feeds and nourishes an entire pollinator network, enabling a multitude of future coriander plants to grow.

In the garden, this shift from plant to flower to seed may happen over a few weeks (it doesn't happen in a single moment), but it is a clearly defined shift and a natural part of the life cycle of the seed. We may be able to continue picking some leaves to eat as the plant goes to flower, but eventually, inevitably, the cycle will be complete. And while the coriander season may be over for now, and the plant itself may be dying and returning to earth, by noticing, appreciating and trusting the process, we allow exponential expansion in the future.

༄

When we've grown a dream or project to fruition and we've taken time to **harvest** and ship the finished product (whatever that may be), there is often a completion phase of the journey — a letting go and allowing, where the dream must shift gears and move on. For us, entering this phase of the journey with our eyes wide open will enable us not only **harvest** the gifts of the dream itself, but to bring with us all of the lessons and seeds that this dream may carry for future dreaming to come.

SAVE YOUR SEEDS

I ate a mandarin orange from one of our citrus trees the other day. It was super juicy and I loved every bite. I was also grateful to have a spare hand while eating it to collect the seeds I found in each bite ... 28 seeds total in the one piece of fruit! Twenty-eight seeds in one mandarin means every time I eat one, I have the potential to plant 28 new mandarin orange trees. The tree I picked this particular mandarin from was a young tree so it may only produce about 10 mandarins this year, but that already means 280 potential new trees could come from this single tree, just this year. If a mature mandarin orange tree produces 100 mandarins in a season, that's 2,800 new potential trees annually from each tree. If the tree fruits abundantly for 10 years, we have the potential to grow 28,000 new mandarin trees (each with its own mandarins and seeds) — all from a single seed that was nurtured to become this one tree.

We roasted a pumpkin last night for dinner. It was a beautiful pumpkin and super nourishing for a winter's evening meal. Again, I was grateful to have a bowl next to me while I was cutting up the pumpkin in prep for the oven, because there were about 100 seeds inside the one pumpkin. These are now drying out in the garden cottage for planting next season. The vine this pumpkin came from had five other pumpkins growing on it, each of those with approximately 100 seeds inside. Do the maths on these seeds, and from a single vine in one season, we'll have seeds for 500 more vines to grow five pumpkins each, producing 250,000 pumpkin seeds by year two.

Wow!

Each single coriander flower produces hundreds of coriander seeds (thousands from each plant). From each mustard green, hundreds of pods will form, each filled with a whole handful of seeds. Inside each avocado is the seed of a new tree. Inside each mango are pods of seeds for many more. All seeds that grow to flower and fruit bring with them seeds that carry the blueprint and capacity for future generations.

❧

Not every seed will grow into a new tree but are you getting the picture? And how this applies to your dream?

A single dream seed brought to fruition brings gifts of its own, while creating seeds for many future dreams to come.

❧

Because plants and trees don't walk or fly, they rely on animals, humans, the wind and the rain to help carry their seeds out into the world to be planted. Not all seeds make it to fertile ground, not all seeds are given the right conditions to grow. As a gardener, you would need a whole lot of land to be able to expand your mandarin orchard by 28,000 trees while adding 250,000 pumpkins in a year.

What's more, these seeds, plants, flowers and fruit learn and evolve along the way. As seasons pass and plants adapt to their growing environment, each new generation evolves its chemistry to be more resilient, more productive, more ready for the next season's growth to come. A kale seed that struggles in year one will produce seeds that are more equipped to handle the same conditions in the following season. Over time, seeds not only grow, they also learn how to grow even better next time.

And they learn to grow for us. I've read stories of gardeners in Russia who hold each seed in the palm of their hand (or in their mouth) for a period of time before it is planted so that their seeds are imprinted with the deep intention and health needs of the grower and have a chance to draw upon nature and respond. I've also read research of honey from bees carrying the exact antibodies that their beekeepers need to treat specific

*medical conditions, indicating a dynamic exchange of information
between the keeper, the bee and the flowers that provide the nectar for
their honey.*

❧

There is a lot that we don't know and may never understand fully
with our minds about the intricacies of nature, but one thing that is
undeniably true is that we are all connected. Because of this, the more we
can tune our own rhythms and actions in with the rhythms and patterns
of the natural world around us, the more we will discover gifts and
lessons in every season and stage of the journey.

With the completion of each life cycle of a single seed grown to fruition
(in the form of a head of lettuce, herb bush, pumpkin vine or fruit tree),
comes with it not only the gift of the fruit and leaves we initially set
out to grow, but also many seeds to grow many more similar (and even
better) plants to fruition in the future.

In the same way, each time we nurture one dream to completion in our
lives, with it comes multiple seeds for future dreams and projects to grow.

Inside each story that is written exists the inklings and characters of
many other tales. Inside each travel adventure exists the inspiration to
go again and visit all the places we didn't get to explore. As one business
venture goes to market, it becomes a wellspring of tributary ideas for
future development.

CHOP AND DROP: THE GIFT OF DYING DREAMS

When the garden greens have bolted to flower and the flowers have turned to seed and when the seeds have all be been collected for next year's garden, there is a final step that not only puts your seedling dream to rest, but allows it to give back to the very soil that held and nurtured its growth.

At this stage, what once were neat rows of lettuce, kale and mustard greens easily gleaned five minutes before each meal, now look like a rambling tangle of dried stalks and broken stems jutting out in many directions, bending over garden paths and collapsing onto each other. No longer green and growing up. No longer capable of holding their own weight. In this moment, the garden bed looks and feels like chaos. It's not producing fruit, there are no flowers remaining for the bees. It's tired, complete and ready to return to where it came from.

In our efforts to 'tidy' things up, we may be tempted to pull all of these exhausted plants from their surrendered position and cart them out of the garden (and indeed every once in a while a complete churning of the soil is great), but season to season we are learning that if we pull last season's crop out by the roots, we not only cause unnecessary disruption to an entire network of mycelial life below ground, we also deprive the plant from completing its final step and natural impulse to give back.

In most cases, the very best thing to do is simply cut the plants at their base, chop them up a little and let them drop right where they stand to become compost and mulch in the soil that has supported their journey of growth.

There is nothing required from the plant in this moment, but simply to let go. To release its need to grow or produce anything at all and

❧

In our modern days of multi-layered multi-tasking, overlapping projects, goals, objectives and agendas, it can be very easy to go from one project or focus area directly into the next. To finish one season of competition and to start training for the following year on the following day.
To complete one milestone and immediately fix our resolve and attention on the next. Indeed, there can be great benefit in building momentum from one mission to the next, and there are times when opportunity or requirement of seamless transition doesn't allow for a complete 'chop and drop' (i.e., month in Hawai'i, lying on the sand). But this does not delete the fundamental requirement to allow ourselves to fully 'complete' our energetic commitment and connection to one dream before moving on to the next.

Failure to allow ourselves to chop, drop and get complete means we may enter the next dream-growing season with a whole bunch of dried up, tangled remnants of last season's dream still crowding our mind and energy. It means less integration and rejuvenation, less room and growing space for what we may feel truly called to grow next. Even if last season's harvest was abundant, if it is left to stand and take up all the vital growing space, it will block the light and continue drawing nutrients from the soil, instead of giving back.

When we have followed a dream from seed to fruition, when we have given everything we know how to give, when we have breathed life into our ideas with action, follow-through, observation, adaption and devotion — there comes a moment when the only thing that must be done is an act of non-doing. When the dream (or our involvement in it) is complete, a final essential step is to genuinely allow ourselves to let it go.

No matter how significant, successful or challenging your last dream was to grow, if your mind remains cluttered and fixated on last year's dream after it is finished, you won't have the clear space to cultivate the new dream when it comes time to develop and nurture what's next.

GIVE IT SPACE. LET IT GO. LET IT REST.

Ancient Essene texts tell us that the space between our inbreath and our outbreath is where all the secrets of the Universe exist, readily accessible to all who are willing to pause quietly in that space. And so, we can say that in the space between one dream finishing and the next beginning is the opportunity to be still for a moment, to create space for a pause without inhaling or exhaling, without dreaming or doing.

⌘

One of my dreams is to develop skills as a freediver. With origins in pearl diving and spearfishing, freediving is a sport/art that requires expanding our breath-holding capacity and the ability to dive down deep.

I'm not a spearfisherman, pearl diver or adrenalised athlete (anymore). I don't have any desire to break time or depth records in freediving. But I've studied and practised freediving for several years now with the simple goal of being able to rest peacefully for as long as possible 5–15 metres below the water's surface.

Why?

Because this is the approximate depth range that humpback whales hover in when they are resting between breaths. If you have developed this capacity and visit certain parts of the world in certain seasons, you might meet these ancient, gentle giants down there. To connect eye-to-eye underwater with a whale is one of the most profound, expansive experiences I've encountered. So much so that several years ago, I started running annual retreats in the Kingdom of Tonga, bringing small groups of leaders together to swim with humpbacks, as a doorway into a 'deeper' exploration of purpose and calling in life. In decades of coaching and facilitation, I have never met greater guides for such a journey than whales.

With a natural capacity to stay under water for 20–40 minutes, whales are the masters of pausing between the inbreath and the outbreath. One of the by-products of practising freediving as a human, is the gradual increase in our ability to extend this pause for a few minutes at a time. The aim is not to push ourselves to 'hold' our breath longer, but to expand the period of inner quiet where we have no compulsion to breathe. There's a difference.

ભ

Taking a pause in life between the inbreath and outbreath of a dream can likewise be one of the most powerful gifts of 'non-doing' we can give to ourselves and the future dreams that are waiting to grow from deep within. And, similar to breathwork and freediving, this pause can feel uncomfortable.

As winter gives way to spring, as summer gives way to autumn, as day gives way to night, in the space between seasons, our garden of seeds and dreams is given natural moments of pause. There are times when it wouldn't matter how hard we try or how much we want something to move forward or grow, what is required is simply to be still, to rest, to let the soil of life regather itself, to let the dream sleep.

In the garden, often there is overlap between seasons and it is easy to get into the habit of planting something new just as the last thing is finishing up. If we are in tune with the seasons and cycles of growth on our land, we will be thoughtful about how we rotate what goes in each garden bed, giving areas that need it time to fully **rest** and rejuvenate.

Conceptually, we understand the need for rest and stillness, and we have all experienced the fresh power that can emerge from a quiet space between projects, seasons or key phases of work. We know these moments of pause can infuse our entire being with fresh perspective, energy and clarity. We know that when we step away and take even a few deep breaths, we literally perceive and experience our reality differently. However, amidst the driving rhythms of modern life, many of us find resting in the power of stillness to be the most difficult step of all — perhaps because no doing is required!

But if we genuinely knew that the quality, clarity and expanse of our *next step* in life was in direct proportion to the quality and depth of rest and recovery we gain following the *last step*, how would we approach this space between breaths in our dream-growing journey?

Amazingly, even taking time to slow down our breathing for two minutes—something we know can have a quantum impact on how we feel and perform on all levels—is something we very easily forget, postpone or bypass.

We convince ourselves that we don't have time to take 10 deep breaths because we need to use the next two minutes to do more stuff — even though the stuff we want to do, if we want to do it well, is going to require every bit of oxygen we can give it.

Let's interrupt that pattern — right now, please. Let's stop for a moment and prove to ourselves and each other how easy and effective it can be to pause for a moment, to **rest** all this seed planting and dream growing, and simply breathe. Right now, let's sit up a little taller and relax our face and shoulders for a moment. I'd love you to actually do this, even if you're in a place where people might wonder what you are doing. Let's just slow it all down for a moment and let them wonder. For a couple of minutes, as you're reading this, focus your energy on slowing and deepening your breath. Nothing unnatural or forced, just a bit deeper and a bit slower and a bit more powerful than normal. Inhale for five seconds … Pause at the top … Exhale for six to seven seconds … Pause at the bottom … And again. That's it, just like that. Deep, full long, slow breaths. Fill your whole body. Feel it full. Then empty your whole body and feel it empty. And repeat. Now stop reading and just breathe like this for a couple minutes… Then pause and notice how you feel. Notice how the space inside your body feels and how the room you are sitting in feels. Different? More expansive? More grounded? More present? I'm feeling it even as I type the words!

At base, this is what I mean by taking time to pause. This is as simple and profound as it is. This pause between dreams may be as short as a few minutes or as long as a season. The most important part is to notice when it comes and to honour it.

When we pause and **rest** in the soil of our being, we not only give ourselves the gift of time to think and see and dream anew, but we also signal to Life that we trust the natural rhythms of the seasons and the way things grow, evolve, live, die and re-emerge. In the pause between breaths, we have the opportunity to come into deep alignment with our own true nature and the natural world. And we remember that, ultimately, these two things are one in the same.

Times are urgent.
Let us slow down.

NIGERIAN PROVERB

WE GROW OUR DREAMS, OUR DREAMS GROW US

In my work with leaders and teams, it is very clear for me to see how the steps required to complete one project not only lead the group to achieve the intended outcome, but these steps also produce hundreds of lessons, fresh impulses, new ideas, personal breakthroughs and 'a-ha!' moments that contribute to the growth of the dream builders in the process.

Amidst the efforts required to build and grow an aspirational project, comes the equal requirement for the humans to grow along with it. If the humans are growing, we will have a chance to create something new and pioneering. If the humans are clinging to how they've always done things, then whatever they create will be a slight variation or incremental improvement (at best) from what has been achieved in the past.

As we develop our dreams, we are constantly being developed by them. The bigger the dream, the more requirement and opportunity for growth. The more experienced we become, the more we tend to lean on our experience to define the path before us. As we evolve our dream, we will need to find the balance between bringing everything we know to the table and simultaneously challenging ourselves to be humble enough to step beyond what we know, into new territory. We gather teams and funding and build bold plans and visions to help the dream grow. But what if the whole reason the dream existed in the first place was actually to help us grow?

I have had the gift of participating, contributing and supporting the growth of many inspired projects, teams and dreams that I would say have deep intrinsic value (noble causes, pioneering visions, humanitarian and environmental missions). But when the project is over and the *harvest* is complete, if you ask me, the most profoundly important thing of all has been the growing, awakening and harvesting of people along the way.

When the dream is finished, this is what remains — the expanded human, with new reference points for what is possible and new capacity to see and dream beyond. We are waking up, building this capacity, both individually and collectively, to dream and create at new levels in the world. This is perhaps the greatest gift of the dream. It is helping us remember who we really are.

♋

A few years ago, I was working with the leaders of a giant capital project involving thousands of engineers and multiple building companies from around the world coming together to construct a very complex processing plant. The project director was a very serious man under an immense amount of pressure to tightly manage the cost, schedule and safety of the workforce while delivering a world-class project to the shareholders. Every time I visited the project we would go for a walk and often he would talk the entire time, venting a complex web of frustrated angst and focused determination around the countless details, technical hurdles and team members not pulling their weight. I would ask a few questions and mostly listen. Somehow, by the end of our walk and his rant, he would take a deep breath, exhale the last of it and smile for a moment. He'd thank me for being there, say he felt much better and then he'd march back into battle. It was a funny cycle. During our last visit together, right near the end of the project, he was quiet for almost the entire walk. Barely said a word, then he paused at the end and looked at me with a tear in his eye.

"You know, I've been working on this project for about 15 per cent of my life now." This was a strange thing to consider. "Seven and a half

years full of details, processes, spread sheets and arguments—so many arguments—that all seemed so important at the time."

He paused, looking out over the giant construction area. "But when I look back, I can tell you right now, I won't remember a single nut or bolt. Not a single piece of equipment or fight I tried to win. The only thing I will remember are a very small handful of special moments I shared with people."

He smiled to himself and shook his head, "Seven and a half years of stress and focus with only a handful of meaningful moments ... that's probably not enough." He shook my hand and grabbed my shoulder for a moment before heading back into his office. "I'll do better next time."

❧

Business ventures come and go, Olympic medals and world championships mark a moment in time, and each of these are worth building towards, fighting for, growing with and celebrating in full. But when the season's shift and flowers go to seed, what we are left with and what we bring with us is the growth, lessons and realisations we have gathered with us along the way.

The business outcome or Olympic medal is the fruit of our **harvest**, but the seeds of future successes are found in the expanded awareness, deepened resolve, honed confidence and relationships we have developed during the journey. The dream will come and go, but the growth of our perspective, capacity, philosophy and approach will stay with us as we move on. Amidst achieving great things on the outside, the seeds of growth we plant on the inside are what will remain in days and years to come.

*When my dream as an athlete came to completion, it brought with it the
seeds of insight and energy to fuel a lifelong journey as a coach.
When my loving connection with Ash grew to a peak, it allowed us
to create another human (Josh) which ignited our lifelong journey as
parents. As the process of writing this book comes to a close, I get to
witness and take part in the transformation of a personal project into a
tangible offering to be shared with many. I am grateful for the growing
this process has required of me, deepening my connection to my garden
and my dreams, awakening in me fresh creative seeds for other books and
projects to grow. Seeds of new dreams, initiatives and friendships that
may never have emerged had I not taken the time and energy to nurture
this one to fruition.*

℘

Each dream we commit to brings with it seeds of future possibilities
often unseen until we have been on the journey, nurtured the seedling to
fruition and given ourselves the great gift of growing alongside it.
It is here in the resting place where, for a moment, we can breathe in and
out, without the need to do anything else but integrate the journey we
have been on.

WE NEED YOUR DREAMS. THANK YOU.

There are many changes happening on the planet, many challenges that we must find the courage to face and navigate together. One of which is that we have become very disconnected from the natural world around us. We have lost the sense of co-creative harmony that many of our native ancestors carried in their way of living and working with the land.

We have lost our connection to seeds.

And with it, amidst the many pressures and stresses of the world around us, we have stopped allowing ourselves to dream. We have censored our passions and curbed our visions in ways that are keeping us way smaller than we came here to be.

We have lost our connection to dreams.

I believe there has never been a more important, compelling, and exciting time to grow both our gardens and our dreams. My deep intention is that this book has helped you commit to doing more of both.

Each of us have special skills and insight that are needed. Each of us have unique dreams that only we carry the seeds to. By awakening these aspects of ourselves in action we are adding our seeds to a global garden of inventive, creative, inspired possibility that we and the world truly needs. And by working with the soil and the earth in a very real and grounded way (sleeves up, hands in), our sense of connection to the pulse of life and what's truly needed grows naturally day by day. Breath by breath. Seed by seed.

As we each start planting more seeds into the earth (and following the steps to have our gardens thrive) and as we each start growing more true dreams in our lives (and following the steps to enable these visions to flourish), a vast majority of the issues we face will surely dissolve,

transform and move powerfully in the direction of new balance
and harmony.

The fundamental aim of this book has been to help re-awaken *your*
connection to the importance of *your* dreams, as a foundational
prerequisite for the positive future of life on Earth.

We need your dreams.

We need you thriving. Because when you're thriving, when you are
throwing back the sheets to dive into your dream each day, you bring
immense creative power into the world with you. The way you see
the world creates new possibility. The way you move in the world
moves mountains.

Wherever you are in your own garden and dream-growing journey, thank
you for taking time to bring yourself to these pages, to contemplate,
cultivate, listen and take bold action in the service of the dreams that are
in you now, ready to be planted and nurtured to fruition.

*Thank you for being here in the garden of life and for planting the seeds of
your dreams into the world.*

I look forward to seeing you out there in the wide-open field of all
possibility.

Let's go!

REFLECTION

- What is one dream, vision or project you have completed this year that you are now ready to genuinely release and put to rest?

- What would it look like for you to create a 'pause between breaths' and actually give yourself space to *be* between dreams, between action and responsibilities in the world — even for a few minutes?

- What are the risks or potential consequences of never really stopping?

- What are the potential benefits of pausing with deep intent to integrate your journey and open yourself to dream bigger in the future?

ACTION

1. Rest
2. Reflect
3. Breathe
4. Begin again

This is the beginning of a day
full of infinite potential.

This is a moment both ripe
with fruit to harvest and alive
with rich soil and fresh seeds
to plant.

You are the master gardener
in this field, and you are
working in direct communion
with all of Life.

This is your garden to grow,
and Life has prepared you to
arrive at this moment — in
this season, at the perfect
time, in perfect rhythm with
the great forces of nature.

Smile deeply and move with
quiet confidence.

Step with grace and power
into the fullness of your
dreams.

GRATITUDE

Sow seeds of love wherever you go, and see them grow and flower and flourish.

Seeds of love sown in even the hardest of hearts will start to grow in the end; it may take time for the seeds to germinate, but as they are tended with loving care, they cannot fail to grow.

EILEEN CADDY

Looking back now, I can see that the seeds of this book have been growing in the soil of my being since the very beginning.

I give thanks to my grandfather Pops — a wild dreamer and the first grower of seeds I ever knew.

I give thanks to my Mom and Dad. You have both, in your own way, completely honoured me as a person and supported the dreams of our family at every phase of life. What a gift.

I give thanks to my brothers for our constant and ever-evolving friendship. Ten thousand moments of laughter, reflection, insight and encouragement. I love you both tons.

I am grateful for all of the coaches, teammates, clients, athletes, artists and leaders I have had the gift of spending time with. You continually expand my view of what is possible and help evolve my understanding of what it takes to nurture the seed of a dream or vision into full fruition in the world.

For your contribution to the growing of our garden and bee apiary, I give thanks to Joel Orchard, Mahto von Schlippe, Willow Hankinson, Gail Joy Shepard and all of the friends and family members who have spent time with hands and feet in the soil — preparing, digging, planting, watering, weeding, harvesting and loving the soil, trees and bees here on our land. Your lifetime membership includes garden harvest or honey on every visit.

For your support in the cultivation of this special project, I give thanks to my dear friend Amir Piass for kindly holding me accountable to "deliver" chapters, to Zenaya Sol for your insightful reflections (on gardens and dreams!) in the first finished manuscript, to Toni Carmine Salerno, Jules Sutherland and the whole Blue Angel Publishing team for your partnership and energy to bring this seed to fruition.

For inspiring me daily and creating the garden of our precious life together, I give my whole heart of gratitude to Ash and Josh. You two are the greatest seeds of all.

For the insight reflected in these pages and the profound lessons available in every moment, I give thanks to the divine force of Nature. Your presence, power, wisdom and grace is the source of all seeds and the greatest teacher on Earth.

We are all seeds growing in the great garden of life. I am grateful to be here, to have a chance to learn, connect, plant and grow … and to share our harvests together.

Whatever you can do, or
dream you can, begin it.
Boldness has genius,
power and magic in it.

JOHANN WOLFGANG VON GOETHE

ABOUT THE AUTHOR

CHIP RICHARDS

As a former elite athlete whose Olympic dream took a radical turn through injury at the peak of his sporting career, Chip Richards has spent most of his life devoted to exploring human potential and supporting the path of purpose with individuals, teams and projects globally. As a coach and mentor working closely with the dreams of athletes, artists, founders and leaders of many walks, Chip has gained a deep appreciation for the steps and phases required to bring bold visions and callings to life. As a passionate gardener, beekeeper, surfer and freediver, he has also developed deep reverence for the patterns and cycles of nature, and what they have to teach us.

While Chip's work currently brings him into the heart of some of the world's largest and most pioneering projects and organisations, increasingly he finds himself venturing with these leaders and teams into immersive experiences in the natural world — as a doorway to true clarity, connection and breakthrough. Chip and his family live in the hinterland of Byron Bay, Australia, on a small, lush acreage surrounded by fruit trees, vegetable gardens, flowering herbs and the hum of bees — all of which were planted and welcomed there as 'seeds of a dream'.

To learn more about Chip's work, please visit ***www.chiprichards.global***

More from
Blue Gaia World Publishers:

BUDDHISM:
THE SCIENCE OF
PEACE & HAPPINESS

Lama Tendar and Ani Dechen

Welcome to a realm of tranquillity and insight, as you explore the timeless wisdom of Tibetan Buddhism. Immerse yourself in a 52-card deck and a full-colour guidebook containing the secrets of inner peace and boundless happiness. Crafted by a revered Buddhist lama and nun, this unique deck offers a no-nonsense, scientific approach to meeting life's challenges with compassion and clarity.

Each card distils centuries of wisdom into practical guidance, empowering you to integrate these profound teachings into your daily life. With every draw, you'll nurture the art of happiness through direct experience, deep understanding, and boundless kindness, benefiting not only yourself but all sentient beings.

Prepare to unlock the secrets to a harmonious existence and embark on a transformative journey towards a compassionate, insightful and fulfilling life.

ISBN: 978-1-922574-02-2
52 circular cards +128-page full-colour guidebook.

For more information on this or any
Blue Gaia World Publishers˚ release,
please visit our website:

www.bluegaiapublishing.com